TRAINING THE TRAINER
PERFORMANCE-BASED TRAINING
FOR TODAY'S WORKPLACE

TRAINING THE TRAINER
PERFORMANCE-BASED TRAINING FOR TODAY'S WORKPLACE

Mary Jo Dolasinski

With Contributing Editors

Anna Graf Williams
Karen J. Hall

Upper Saddle River, NJ 07458

Library of Congress Cataloging-in-Publication Data

Dolasinski, Mary Jo.
  Training the trainer : performance-based training for today's workplace / Mary Jo
Dolaskinski ; consulting editors, Anna Graf Williams, Karen J. Hall.
     p. cm.
  Includes index.
  ISBN 0-13-042343-2
   1. Employees--Training of. 2. Employee training personnel--Training of. I. Williams,
Anna Graf. II. Hall, Karen J. III. Title.

HF5549.5T7D567 2003
658.3'12404--dc21   2002038168

Editor-in-Chief: *Stephen Helba*
Executive Editor: *Vernon R. Anthony*
Director of Manufacturing and Production:
   Bruce Johnson
Managing Editor: *Mary Carnis*
Production Editor: *Adele M. Kupchik*
Executive Assistant: *Nancy Kesterson*
Editorial Assistant: *Ann Brunner*
Development Editor: *David Morrow*
Desktop Publisher: *Karen J. Hall/George D.*
   Williams
Copy Editor: *Cheryl Pontius*

Interior Design/Formatting: *Learnovation®, LLC*
Proofreader: *Barbara Cassell*
Manufacturing Buyer: *Cathleen Petersen*
Creative Director: *Cheryl Asherman*
Cover Coordinator/Design: *Christopher*
   Weigand
Electronic Art Creation: *Alison St. Claire*
Marketing Manager: *Ryan DeGrote*
Marketing Assistant: *Elizabeth Farrell*
Marketing Coordinator: *Adam Kloza*
Printer/Binder: *Phoenix Book Tech*

Pearson Education LTD.
Pearson Education Australia PTY, Limited
Pearson Education Singapore, Pte. Ltd
Pearson Education North Asia Ltd
Pearson Education Canada, Ltd
Pearson Educación de Mexico, S.A. de C.V.
Pearson Education -- Japan
Pearson Education Malaysia, Pte. Ltd

10 9 8 7 6 5 4 3 2 1
ISBN 0-13-042343-2

CONTENTS

Preface   xv

Training Today   xv
　Who Should Read This Book?   xv
　Training is Changing   xvi
　Learning is Performance   xvi

The Chapters   xviii

About the Author   xxi

Dedication   xxii

Acknowledgments   xxii

Chapter 1 – Training Today   1

The New Workplace   2
　A New Business Model   2
　Technology   3

The New Work Force   3
　Training That Makes an Impact   4
　Making Training Stick   4
　Capturing Audience Attention   5

Training is Performance   6

Reference   9

Skill Builders   9

Chapter 2 – Why Do You Need Training?   11

Training as a Strategic Business Partner   12
　Turning Business Needs into Training Storylines   12
　Creating a Proposal   13
　When Training Is the Answer   14

When Training is NOT the Answer   14
　Problem Solving   15

Needs Analysis   16
    Getting Started   16
    Steps in the Needs Analysis   17

Deciding on the Storyline   20

Creating Measurable Goals   20

Writing Measurable Learning Objectives   21

Set the Standards of Performance   23

Measurement Requires a Plan   24
    Types of Measurement   26
    Write It or Buy It   31

Traditional Instructional Design   32
    Sample Traditional Instructional Design Model   32

Skill Builders   35

Chapter 3 – You as the Actor   37

Role of the Actor   38

Communicating with Your Audience   38
    Your Words   39
    Delivering Your Lines   40
    Have a Good Vocabulary   41
    Your Actions   42
    Appearance   44
    Listening to Your Audience   45

Behaviors that Impact Learning   47

Know Your Material   49

Skill Builders   50

Chapter 4 – The Audience   53

Identify the Audience   54

How People Learn   54
    Adult Learning Principles   54
    Getting "Buy-In" from the Learner   55

Demographics   56
    Cultural Background   56

Experience Level and Position in Company   57
Generational Differences   58

Reference   60

Skill Builders   60

Chapter 5 – Developing the Script, Part 1: The Outline   61

The Script   62
Developing the Content Outline   65

Brainstorming Your Content   65
Creative Brainstorming Techniques   65

Organizing Your Information   68
Review Training Goals and Objectives   69

Creating an Outline   70
Use Subject Matter Experts   73

Making the Training Schedule   74
Energy Levels   76
Finding Time for Training   77

Types of Training   79
One-on-One Training   79
Self-Directed or Individual Development Training   81
Training Moments   82
Training Through Technology   82
Group Training   83

Off the Shelf Training   85

References   86

Skill Builders   86

Chapter 6 – Developing the Script, Part 2: Elements of the Performance   89

Create Mini-Lessons   90

Engaging the Audience   93
Audience-Centered Techniques   93
The Flow of the Performance   95

A Guide to A/V Equipment   96
Low-tech A/V Equipment   97

High-tech A/V Equipment   99

Make Training Fun   103
Use Brainteasers and Mental Stretching Exercises   103
Have Candy on Hand   103
Use Props   104
Bring Toys   105
Use Animated Videos   105
Use Humor in Your Training   106
Use Interactive Storytelling   107

Creative Training Ideas   108
Creative Thinking Techniques   109

Games and Activities   110
Games   110
Activities   112
Audience Size   113

Opening and Closing the Session   113
The Opening   114
Closing the Session   117

When You Get Stuck During Scripting   119

Reference   120

Skill Builders   120

Chapter 7 – Developing the Script, Part 3: Creating the Props   121

The Audience Script   122

The Actor's (Trainer's) Script   125
Script Layout   125
Windowpanes   126
Using Graphics or Icons   127
Outside Facilitators   128

Preparing to Use Technology   129
Flip Charts   129
PowerPoint® or Overhead Transparency Slides   129
Videos   130

Ethics in Training   131

Reference   131

Skill Builders   131

Chapter 8 – Setting the Stage   133

Scheduling the Performance   134
Choosing a Date   134

Selecting the Stage   134
The Facility's Location   135
Type of Facility   135

The Training Room (Your Stage)   136
Stage Capacity   136
Stage Layout   137
Stage Color   137
Stage Decor   138
Stage Lighting   138

Stage Setup (Room Setup)   139
Table Types   139
Setup Types   140
Audio/Visual Needs   142
Technology   144
Food and Beverage   144

Designing Marketing Materials for Your Training   145

Audience Logistics   148
Notifying the Audience   148

Contracts   150

Tracking Attendance   151
Registration Process   152
Master List   152
Post-Performance Responsibility   154

Skill Builders   154

Chapter 9 – Dress Rehearsal   155

Getting Yourself Ready to Perform   156
Personal Preparation   156
Mental Preparation   156
Prepare Yourself Physically   160

Manage the Environment   163
Use Your Space   164

Experiential Levels 164
The "Parking Lot" 164

Performance Day 165
Performance Day Checklist 166

Co-performing 167

Skill Builders 167

Chapter 10 – The Performance   169

Performance—Live and On Stage 170
Greet the Audience 170
Handling the Jitters 170
Ask the Audience Questions 171

The Occasional Distraction 172
In and Out Thinking 172
Be Flexible 173

Conflicts During the Performance 173
Troubleshooting the Classroom 174

Multiple-Day Performances 175
Stop, Start, Continue 175
Daily Closings 176

References 177

Skill Builders 177

Chapter 11 – The Reviews   179

So...How Well Are You Doing? 180
Measuring Training 180
Measurement Today 182

Performance-Based Perspective 182
Cycle of Performance-Based Training 182
Link to the Business Strategy and Goals 183
Identify the Learning Objectives and Set the Performance Standards 184
Train for Success on the Standards 185
Measuring Performance Against the Standard 185
Recognize Success 188
Coaching Opportunities 189

Compare Results to Business Goals   189
Focus on Continuous Feedback   190
Intangible Measures   192
When the Training is Complete   193

Return on Investment   193
ROI Defined   193
The Goal of ROI   194
The Challenges of ROI   194

Calculating ROI   195
The Costs   195
The Savings   196
Net Program Benefits   197
The Calculation   197

References   199

Skill Builders   200

Chapter 12 – E-Learning Basics   201

Training with Technology   202

What is E-Learning?   202
Benefits of E-learning   203
Challenges of E-learning   203

Is E-learning for You?   204

Designing E-Learning   207
Internal or External Development   207
Designing Instruction   207
Structuring E-learning   209

The Future of E-learning   210
New Technology Trends   210

Tech Terms   212

References   214

Skill Builders   214

Appendix A – Resources - Books, Periodicals, and Others   215

Books   215

Periodicals to Check Out   218

Digital Stock Photography   218

Music   218

Video   219

Cartoons   219

_____

Appendix B – On-Line Resources   221

Book and Binder Vendors   221

On-Line Learning Companies   221

Cool Web Sites   222

Resources for On-Line Info on On-Line Learning Design   222

Software Companies   223

Companies for Promotional Items/Training Aids   223

Video Vendors   223

Organizations to Check Out   224

For Information on Games, Check Out These Web Sites   224

_____

Appendix C – Training Tip on Copyrights   225

_____

Appendix D – The New Training Room   227

How We Learn   227
   Lucid Dreaming   227
   Tele-immersion   227
   Virtual Retinal Display   228
   Digital Pedagogy   228
   Extras   228

_____

Appendix E – Writing a Proposal   231

Writing a Proposal   231

Part One: The Description   231

Part Two: The Financial Impact   232

Part Three: The ROI   233

Glossary   235

Index   243

PREFACE

TRAINING TODAY

Training today is a strategic investment into a future where attracting and retaining employees is a part of the business plan, and technology significantly impacts the way we live, communicate, and work. Our past suggested many of our work environments were that of manual labor. Now many of those same work environments are fueled by technology. We have shifted to a thinking and service economy. Work teams, career banding, career latticing, and career circles have replaced traditional individual job descriptions, organizational charts, and career ladders.

Training in the 21st century demands trainers who have a broad set of skills–from motivation to financial management, from performance to project management. This changing perspective is requiring a new training model. The trainer is now a strategic business partner, a business partner that can help companies develop their employees.

Today's training professionals are continually faced with the challenges of preparing people for new roles, helping redesign people practices, and supporting and driving the corporate culture. Today, uncertainty has caused us to change the way we teach, what we teach, and how we teach it.

Who Should Read This Book?

This book was written for anyone interested in furthering his or her abilities to teach, train, and enhance knowledge including:

- Trainers/training professionals (new and experienced)
- Directors of training
- Teachers/educators wanting to learn new approaches in the classroom
- Managers/leaders/supervisors who do training
- Subject matter experts who need to do training.

Training is Changing

Businesses are starting to realize that when people and their processes are aligned, profits follow. Companies are looking for business partners who can develop their employees in an ever-changing and uncertain business climate.

This book provides you with a plan to be successful in this constantly changing workplace. It simplifies the notion of training, and the information is presented in a useful, retainable, timely, and fun way.

Over the last 20 years as a teacher and training professional I have watched as the environment of the classroom has evolved. We have gone from a formal environment to a more relaxed and casual environment. Students want to learn, they just learn differently from those before them. Today, more than ever, the teacher or trainer has to "be on."

Learning is Performance

Today's learners learn best when they are relaxed and enjoying themselves. They also learn more when we can stimulate both the analytical and the creative sides of their brain. Ultimately, training is like a stage performance–providing education in such a way that engages the audience in new and exciting ways.

In the spirit of this performance, we need to look at ourselves sometimes as the playwright (writing the training materials), and sometimes as the actor on stage (the trainer), trying to get our message across. The tools we have to help us include the effective use of our script (training materials), our stage (anywhere we are conducting training), our audience (our trainee), and our ability to use our skills to perform effectively.

The purpose of this book is to provide you with a road map for successful training in our constantly changing workscape. The goal of the book is to simplify the notion of training and present information to you in a useful, retainable, timely, and fun way that can easily be applied. To this end, there are several features in the book to help you navigate including:

Trainer Terms – definitions of words or phrases used in training.

Subject Matter Expert (SME) – someone who has expert knowledge about a given topic or given skill

Trainer Pitfalls – designed to highlight common mistakes made in training. Solutions are offered as well.

Trainers assume the audience can always see the personal benefits of attending training. This is not always the case. Great trainers help their audience visualize how the training will help them accomplish a goal, increase their earning potential, or learn a new skill.

Highlight Boxes – short facts and statements related to the topic in that chapter or section.

FYI . . .

Today's learner learns best in short sittings, 1-2 hours, with activities.

Creative Ideas – highlighting ideas to enhance training and add creativity to its application.

At the close of a session, ask audience members to write one question they think everyone in the class should be prepared to answer which is specific to the training they just received. Collect the questions and read them aloud for an instant review. Note: This technique can also be used throughout the session as well as to collect a base for future written evaluations.

Pullout Boxes – reinforce key concepts within the chapter or section.

Your script should include:

- Goals
- Measurable learning objectives
- Standards of performance expected from your audience that support the learning objectives
- Specific directions on how to deliver or perform the script.

THE CHAPTERS

Chapter One - Training Today

Offers a summary of how the workplace and its work force are changing. It discusses how training and training professionals have to change to meet the needs of the new learner. Ultimately, great training is performance.

Chapter Two - Why Do You Need Training?

Examines when to use training as a solution. Performing a needs analysis and developing program goals and objectives are discussed.

Chapter Three - You as the Actor

Discusses the integral role the trainer as actor plays in the learning process. It further explores presentation techniques for effective presentation and communication.

Chapter Four - The Audience

Deals with the audience — planning for different types of people, viewing how people learn, and learning what motivates the audience.

Chapter Five - Developing Your Script - Part 1: The Outline

Designed to teach the basics of how to go from training ideas to a detailed training outline. Also looks at various training methods.

Chapter Six - Developing Your Script - Part 2: Elements of the Performance

Focuses on taking the detailed training outline and working on the flow of the performance, planning for activities, games, and audio visuals. Planning the opening and closing of the sessions is also covered.

Chapter Seven - Developing Your Script - Part 3: Creating the Props

Concentrates on developing the written materials, audio visuals, and handouts used in the training performance.

Chapter Eight - Setting the Stage

Deals with the "nuts and bolts" of a performance—from who is attending to where to have it and every logistic in between.

Chapter Nine - Staging and The Dress Rehearsal

Focuses on the preparation of a performance. This chapter explores both the mental and physical preparation required for success.

Chapter Ten - The Performance

Looks at classroom management issues during the actual training session. How to work the room, how to deal with difficult people, how to handle emergencies.

Chapter Eleven - The Reviews

Measurement and evaluation are the heart of this chapter. Kirkpatrick's four levels of evaluation are discussed, as well as thinking outside the "evaluation box."

Chapter Twelve - E-Learning Basics

Explores the new technologies available in the training arena, focusing on electronic learning: what it is, what it can do, and how to design training. The chapter also looks at new trends in training uses for technology.

Appendixes

Includes lists of resources available in the training arena, detailed information on measurement techniques, proposal writing and return on investment.

This book is written to help you take the building blocks of performance-based training and to own them for yourself. It is the hope of this author you will learn new concepts and methods for the training you conduct in today's workplace. Remember to honor the traditional training model while customizing your own performance-based training style.

ABOUT THE AUTHOR

Mary Jo Dolasinski has a bachelor's of science degree in Hospitality and Tourism Management and a master's degree in Communication and Creative Arts. She has been training and teaching in both industry and academia for more than 15 years. As corporate director of Training and Career Development for White Lodging Services, she is responsible for all activities related to management and employee training. In this role she has developed and implemented company-wide initiatives such as New Hire Orientation, Certification Training, Leadership Training, Ongoing Development programs, etc. She has also developed partnerships with Marriott International, state government, and community-based organizations to implement training in such areas as Welfare to Work, Career Advancement Training for the company's incumbent, and Work Specific English to help immigrant employees.

Mary Jo serves as a national trainer for Marriott International, conducting training classes for managers and supervisors across the country on topics including: how to conduct training, time management and managing change. She has been a guest lecturer for Purdue University's Calumet campus for the last 10 years teaching small-group communication and public speaking, as well as a host of hospitality, management, and human resource classes.

Over the last several years, Mary Jo's efforts have been recognized nationally, including White Lodging Services' recognition as one of the Top 100 Training Companies for 2002 as determined by *Training Magazine*. She received the Industry Recognition Award for ongoing efforts toward the advancement of hospitality and tourism education presented by International Council of Hotel, Restaurant and Institutional Education Association (ICHRIE) and was recognized as a "Best Practice Champion" in American Lodging Excellence by the American Hotel and Lodging Association.

She has been invited to deliver keynote addresses and workshops for many organizations including: The Government Meeting Planners Association, Indiana Chapter; ICHRIE; League of Cities; Hospitality Business Alliance; and American Hotel and Lodging Association. She has authored several articles, written a chapter on training for the *Essentials of Food Safety and Sanitation*, and co-authored an *Immigrant's Guide to the American Workplace: Making It in America*, Prentice Hall 2003.

Finally, with a sincere belief in giving back to the industry she works in and being an advocate of education, Mary Jo sits on several boards and is a member of many committees including: Hospitality Advisory Committee for Purdue University-Calumet, the Strategic Planning Committee for ICHRIE, Commissioner for Commission on Accreditation of Hospitality Management Programs, Marriott International's Committee for Management University Training, and various School to Work Committees. She has also spearheaded local events for the promotion of the hospitality industry and education of high school teachers, customer service training for many local businesses, workshops with county convention and tourism bureaus, and partnered with the Department of Economic Development in the city of Gary, IN, to initiate a customer service program for local businesses.

DEDICATION

To every person dedicated to the art of teaching and the pursuit of lifelong learning.

ACKNOWLEDGMENTS

There have been many people who have played a role in helping make this book possible. I would like to thank my husband, Dave, and my children, Lise and Brian, for their patience and encouragement; John J. and White Lodging Services for their support and willingness to think "outside the box"; Mike F. from Purdue University-Calumet for starting me down this path so many years ago; Judith Toman, David Hayes, and Duncan R. Dickson for their willingness to review the book and give me helpful input; and finally the Learnovation®, LLC team of Anna Graf Williams, Karen Hall, David Morrow, and George Williams – whose vision, dedication, and perseverance made this more than just a dream, they helped make it a reality.

Training the Trainer
Performance-Based Training for Today's Workplace

Chapter 1

TRAINING TODAY

If you want a return on your investment in people, the first thing you've got to do is invest in them. —Jeffrey Pheffer - Stanford University

IN THIS CHAPTER:

- The New Workplace
- The New Work Force
- Training is Performance
- Skill Builders

THE NEW WORKPLACE

Business and the work environment are constantly changing. Low unemployment, high turnover, and an ever-changing work force are issues faced by management every day. In an effort to stay competitive, companies are moving at the speed of the Internet. Changes in technology over the past 10 years have significantly impacted the way we live, communicate, and work. As our economy has shifted from an industrial, production-oriented focus to a information-based, service-oriented model, training has changed as well. We no longer have months to study the work environment, see a need for training, and then plan, develop, evaluate, and deliver instruction. In today's environment, we must speed up this process to meet the demand.

For the purpose of this book, **training** is defined as **a dynamic process between people that focuses on the exchange of ideas, with a spirit toward learning and continuous improvement.** Training can include teaching a specific work skill, changing the attitudes of people, or helping them learn to better communicate. To be effective, training must focus on the needs of the organization and connect with the people being trained. Put simply, our greatest training challenges are to prepare people for new roles, redesign established practices, and drive company culture. Training in today's workplace is demanding a different set of skills and a new business model for *every* employee.

A New Business Model

In today's environment, businesses are looking for creative and motivated people who can achieve financial success. Attracting and retaining employees has become a key business strategy. Employees are a company's appreciating assets. Companies are now trying to leverage these assets to maximize their **Return on Investment (ROI)**. This new standard requires companies to get into the business of "people development." In today's workplace, training is no longer a "necessary evil." Training is a strategic investment in the company, its people, and its future. Our greatest training opportunity is to change the way we train to include new perspectives and constantly evolving technologies.

Return on Investment (ROI) –
a value developed by comparing the costs of a training program with the benefits received from the training

Technology

The evolution of technology has led to many advances in training methods and delivery. Technology can make training more cost effective. Training can be delivered at the convenience of the learner via the Internet or company intranet.

Advances in technology allow us to:

- Train more people in less time
- Give people from all areas of a company access to training
- Provide on-demand training at the convenience of the learner
- Give the employee control of his or her own learning
- Track employee performance in training
- Provide distance learning, with a trainer in one location and trainees participating via Internet or video conferencing
- Save money on training expenses
- Take advantage of pre-existing training materials
- Deliver content in new, more interactive ways.

THE NEW WORK FORCE

Ultimately, training is an investment in people. The ability to impact the worker and effect change is the goal of all training. To do this well, you need to understand the dynamics of today's work force:

- **Age diversity**–For the first time, four generations of people are working together. Each group brings its own influences and preferences to the workplace.
- **Cultural diversity**–Our immigrant populations are growing exponentially, requiring a change in how we communicate and teach.
- **Different styles of learning**–People learn in many different ways. Training needs to use many different styles to help people connect with the material.
- **Different expectations for training**–People today are looking for learning experiences that are interactive, relevant to their lives, interesting, and delivered in an entertaining style.

Training That Makes an Impact

Training success is dependent on your ability to make an impact on the audience. To meet this challenge, trainers need to start with an understanding of the "basics" of today's learning environment.

- Technology is changing how people learn and how they relate to one another
- Today's worker wants to learn, but the learning experience has to be fun, creative, and appropriate for what they are doing
- People learn best when they are relaxed and enjoying themselves
- People learn more when both the analytical and creative sides of the brain are engaged
- Training that enlists the five senses and engages the heart, soul, and mind of the trainees is more successful.

These basics demand that the trainer must do more than distribute information to be successful. Information needs to be presented in a fun, creative way that taps into the emotions of the audience. Simply put, training that entertains works! **Edutainment** and **trainertainment** are two new words used to describe this type of training.

TRAINER TERMS

Edutainment / Trainertainment – terms used to refer to education and training that has been combined with some type of entertainment element

Making Training Stick

Successful trainers realize while training is important, it is only the beginning of the total learning experience. What people do with the information and what they take back to the workplace, or the **transfer of learning**, is the ultimate measure of success. Training should always be designed and delivered with measurement in mind. The transfer of learning is how you make training stick— or create **"sticky" training**.

TRAINER TERMS

Transfer of Learning – refers to what skills or lessons the trainee takes back to his/her job and applies it or "transfers" the knowledge back to the workplace. It can also refer to transferring learning to his/her personal life as well.

Sticky Training – a new term in training used to describe how well people remember and apply what they learn! It is how well the lessons

Capturing Audience Attention

A critical component in the transfer of learning is capturing the trainees' attention and keeping them engaged throughout the entire training class. An engaged training member is one who learns and remembers the information presented and transfers the new knowledge back into the workplace. In today's society the trainer's challenge of keeping the audience engaged is greater than ever before. If you consider what the trainee's frame of reference is and what the trainer is being compared to, it seems almost scary! The typical trainee has been:

■ Exposed to 150 channels on TV (and there is still a perception there is "nothing on")

■ Exposed to 2 million Web sites

■ Exposed to music videos with images changing every few seconds.[1]

All these have created an expectation in the minds of the trainee. The old rules for presenting information are no longer valid. Standing in front of your audience and reading or presenting long lectures are no longer acceptable. Trainees today have become accustomed to very visual images, which change frequently. In the words of Malcolm Gladwell: "We have become, in our society, overwhelmed by people clamoring for our attention." As a trainer, how are you going to cut through all the noise, captivate your audience, and keep them captivated throughout the entire training performance?"

Many trainers are trying to teach people using methods that worked in the past. Today's trainer must be willing to be flexible and embrace a different training model.

TRAINING IS PERFORMANCE

The bottom line today... effective training is performance. Just as actors have engaged, educated, and entertained audiences for years, trainers need to employ many of the same techniques to deliver great training experiences for today's learner. A closer look shows how simple it is to enhance the idea of traditional training with the elements of the theater.

Just Compare...

Training as Performance	Traditional Training
The Playwright In the theater, the playwright is the person who develops a storyline into a script for the actors to perform. In training, the playwright is the person developing the training topic or the storyline into the training script.	**The Developer** In traditional training, the developer is the person that designs the content or what will be covered in any given training class. In smaller organizations, this may be the director of training.
The Producer The producer in any theatrical production is critical. It is the producer who obtains financial backing for the performance, keeps track of the budget, etc. In today's competitive environment, training needs to be run like a business—from writing proposals for funding to delivering a Return on Investment for the owners. The role of the trainer mirrors the role of the producer in the training experience.	**The Logistics Coordinator** Traditionally focuses on the mechanics of tuition, training costs, materials, salary and wages, room rental, audio/visual, shipping, licensing fees, travel, charge-backs, etc. that surround training.
The Actor As with any great performance, the actor plays an integral role in its success. In the training arena, the trainer has a direct impact on whether people learn and what they learn. The trainer is an actor on the stage of the training performance.	**The Facilitator or Trainer** This is the person who will be delivering the training written by the developer in a training class. In some cases the developer and the trainer are the same person.

Just Compare...

Training as Performance	Traditional Training
The Audience Just as in the theater, the audience members are the people who come to the performance. They are the employees who are the participants in your training performance.	**The Participant** Used to refer to the student or employee who will be attending a traditional training class.
The Storyline All theatrical performances use a script. The very first step in creating this script is determining the storyline, or the idea or topic, that will be woven into a training performance.	**The Training Topic** The topic, concept, or subject that the organization, department, or trainer has identified as a need for training or personal development.
The Script The script is the written story delivered or read by the actors during a performance to bring the story to life. Effective training begins with a training script. This is the way you will get your training topic or story told in your training performance! In the training performance, there is also a second script which is your audience script or workbook.	**Participant Manuals & Facilitator Guides** Traditionally, manuals and guides are used to help the facilitator and the student throughout the class. The facilitator guide outlines the content that needs to be covered by the trainer during the class. Participant manuals serve as a workbook during training and as a reference back in the workplace.
Enhancing the Script Just as technology is revolutionizing the entertainment world, it is redefining and reinventing the way information is communicated in the training performance. Video, activities, and real objects can also be used to enhance training.	**Audio/Visual** Technology in training was historically the use of overhead projectors, slide projectors, and white boards.
The Stage In performance, the stage plays an integral role in telling the story. In training, your stage is the place where you are conducting training. Your effectiveness relies on how well you use your surroundings.	**The Training Room** The classroom or meeting room is also called the training room. This is the place where a facilitator or trainer delivers training to learners.

Just Compare...

Training as Performance	Traditional Training
Setting the Stage The stage plays a key role in creating the right environment to support the story. Every detail from physical space to the audience contributes to the event.	**The Logistics of Training** Logistics deal with the details including: time, place, sign up, registration, room setup, audio/visual, and food and beverage.
The Dress Rehearsal Actors understand they must be physically and mentally prepared. They understand the importance of rehearsal. As the actor in your training performance, you must prepare and rehearse to provide the best possible experience for your audience.	**Preparation** All trainers and facilitators prepare for their training sessions by reviewing material and making notes. Preparing for training would also include getting materials ready, checking logistics, and preparing to present.
The Performance Captivating the audience is the goal of every actor during a performance. How effectively the actor uses the stage, props, and actions impacts the effectiveness of the performance.	**The Training Class** The actual training is conducted by the facilitator or trainer during class. Information is presented to the learners.
The Reviews On opening night, every actor waits for the reviews to come in. In the training performance, the reviews or evaluations help the actor improve.	**The Evaluations** Typically, once the training is complete, facilitators or trainers will conduct a student evaluation. The goal is to get a measurement of student perception with regard to the quality of the training.

Throughout the rest of this book, we will be exploring each of these components that make up a successful performance. We will look at the roles of the actor and audience; the steps to planning, designing and developing a good training performance. We will also be using the new model's terminology. The trainer is now the actor, the learner is the audience, the guides and handbooks are now your scripts, and so on.

FYI . . .
Training that is entertaining works! Sesame Street proved that combining entertainment with education can be very successful!

REFERENCE

1. Millbower, Lenn. "Entertaining Training Presentations: Show-biz Basics that Engage Distracted Learners." ASTD, 2001 Presentation.

SKILL BUILDERS

1. Why do you want to train?

2. Describe the multi-generational work force needs in today's workplace.

3. Explain how the new training model differs from traditional training.

4. How do you know the transfer of learning has taken place?

Chapter 2

WHY DO YOU NEED TRAINING?

There is nothing training cannot do. Nothing is above its reach. It can turn bad morals to good; it can destroy bad principles and recreate good ones; it can lift men to angelship. — Mark Twain

IN THIS CHAPTER:

- **Training as a Strategic Business Partner**

- **When Training is NOT the Answer**

- **Needs Analysis**

- **Deciding on the Storyline**

- **Creating Measurable Goals**

- **Writing Measurable Learning Objectives**

- **Set the Standards of Performance**

- **Measurement Requires a Plan**

- **Traditional Instructional Design**

- **Skill Builders**

TRAINING AS A STRATEGIC BUSINESS PARTNER

Training is a part of every organization. As we discussed earlier, successful training plays a key role in a company's business plan. Training needs to be matched to the organizational goals, themes and "hot buttons" of the company. In addition to looking at the company's goals, you need to focus on current issues facing the company. Successful training fits into and supports the entire business plan for the organization.

Turning Business Needs into Training Storylines

A **business need** is an identified issue or concern relating to the function or operation of the business. Business needs

TRAINER TERMS

Business Need –
  issue or concern relating to the function or operation of the business

are identified by critically reviewing a company's business plan or by responding to an immediate situation. Once you have identified a business need, you can develop a training solution.

The challenge is to develop specific training solutions that meet the identified business need. Evaluate the business needs you have identified to determine whether or not they can be impacted by training. Once you have determined what the specific business need is, you can begin to develop your storyline. The following grid explains the storyline development process.

The Storyline Development Process:

Step	For Example . . .
1. Identify the business issue.	High employee turnover
2. **Brainstorm** a list of possible challenges, problems, reasons, opportunities, etc., around the issue.	Reasons for high employee turnover may include lack of skills, lack of training, poor communication between management and line-level employees, employees not understanding the standards and expectations, poor hiring decisions/choices, pay levels, etc.

The Storyline Development Process:

3.	Investigate possible **root causes** of the issue.	Conduct an employee opinion survey
4.	Determine causes.	Opinion survey showed: Frustration with the caliber of the people being hired. The new employees seem to have a "don't know, don't care" attitude and aren't capable of doing the job!
5.	Make a list of ways training can be part of the solution.	■ Train management staff on hiring procedures ■ Train management staff on behavioral interviewing techniques ■ Train hourly employees on interviewing techniques so they can be included in hiring process
6.	Once the list is complete, check back with **key stakeholders.**	Submit training topics to managers in the stakeholder departments
7.	Write the **proposal.**	Write a proposal for presenting training classes on the topics

TRAINER TERMS

Brainstorming–
a method of shared problem solving in which all members of a group spontaneously contribute ideas, all are recorded, none are rejected, and ideas build upon each other

Proposal–
a document outlining the training action to be taken to solve a business need

Root Cause –
the main reason a problem exists. It is not always readily evident. It sometimes requires an investigation to get to it.

Key Stakeholders –
any person or persons that directly impact the organization and its success. They include you, the customers, the owners, the managers, and the employees of a given organization.

Creating a Proposal

Proposals are a critical part of the business model. They help to clarify the training process to non-trainers. A proposal is a document outlining the training action to be taken to solve the business need. It is submitted to the management of the company for approval. A good proposal includes an outline of the training to be conducted, justification as to why the training is needed, the targeted audience, the estimated length of training, how it will be conducted, and how much the initiative will cost. See Appendix E for specific details on the proposal writing process.

When Training Is the Answer

When training is the answer, you will need to turn the storyline into a script that can be used to deliver training. Begin the basic storyline by identifying key pieces of content. A quick way to start gathering this information is with a review of what is currently available to you. Start the process with:

- Information gleaned from feedback in the initial analysis
- Company policies
- Best practices in your company and industry
- Training conducted previously on the topic
- Subject matter experts
- Books, magazines, articles, and information taken off the web.

WHEN TRAINING IS NOT THE ANSWER

There are times when training isn't the answer to a problem, situation, or issue. Often managers and supervisors believe training is a cure-all for the issues or "ills" befalling their department. It is not uncommon to be sought out by a manager for a training solution to his or her problem. If training isn't the answer, you may want to help guide the manager in the right direction.

An Example...

You get a call from the restaurant manager. He explains the servers in his restaurant are not getting the customer's food to their tables quickly enough. He tells you they need a training class on customer service. You agree to come and review the situation. After

(continued)

When training is not the answer:

Some examples of **when training is not the answer** include:

- Lack of communication between an employee and a manager
- A non-work related issue
- Attitudinal issues (i.e., the staff knows how to do the activity; they don't want to or refuse to do it.)
- Physical plant issues.

An Example... (continued)

a few minutes in the restaurant, you realize the problem isn't lack of training or knowledge with the servers, but is actually in the kitchen.

Problem Solving

When training is not the answer, you may be asked to help identify what the solution is. The following steps will help you to problem solve.

1. Have the manager or team list issues that are occurring in the department.

2. Identify each issue **as a symptom** of a root cause.

Symptom -
   a symptom is a sign or an indication of disorder, not the root cause of a problem

3. Have members of the team identify potential issues.

4. Have members of the team list solution options.

An Example...

Back to our restaurant manager's problem... you invite him and some of his employees to a brainstorming session. Together they start sharing observations and challenges they have experienced regarding the problem of food not getting to the table in a timely manner. During this brainstorming session they list:

- Cold food
- Meals missing items
- People in the kitchen constantly in the way
- Breakage of plates and glasses
- Lack of communication between servers and the kitchen staff.

You explain to them these are all *symptoms* of the problem. The next step is to identify the *causes*. They list:

- Having to walk from one end of the cooking area to the other to get ingredients
- Not having enough room to work
- Having to hunt down a printout of meal orders

(continued)

An Example...(continued)

■ Not being able to hear each other speak.

From these causes, a picture now begins to form. The way the kitchen is designed, more specifically the way the food line is set up, is hindering the staff from being able to do their jobs effectively and efficiently. Now that the manager has identified the root cause of his problem, he can solve it.

NEEDS ANALYSIS

The best way to determine training needs is to conduct a **needs analysis**. A needs analysis is a study to identify gaps between the current situation and the ideal situation you would like to see in your company. A needs analysis is

TRAINER TERMS

Needs Analysis -
a process used by trainers to identify gaps or needs between the current state and desired state in the organization so that appropriate training can be developed to improve organizational performance

the first thing to consider before undertaking a training project. What problems need to be corrected? Who do you need to connect with to find out the issues? How will you gather the information you need?

Performing a needs analysis doesn't have to be a long drawn-out process. In fact, with the speed of today's business needs, you may find yourself pressured to develop and deliver training as fast as possible. Don't be tempted to skip the process or get caught up in the enthusiasm or excitement of a manager who thinks training will solve all his or her problems without doing a thorough needs analysis. Training not connected to a plan or objective can be costly and ineffective. Needs analysis is a dynamic process with several steps.

Getting Started

Before starting your needs analysis, plan out what you are going to do:

■ **Define what you are looking for—**Are you looking to define problems or opportunities, analyze a specific area or department, or research possible changes?

■ **Identify and interview key stakeholders—**Who will you interview or survey in the organization for information? Keep in mind that feedback may vary from each key stakeholder based on his or her respective individual or departmental needs.

■ **Determine methods of data collection**—Will you use interviews, focus groups, surveys, or a combination of methods to find the issues?

■ **Estimate timelines**—Determine at the beginning how much time you will take conducting the analysis: how long your interviews will be, how much time you will spend analyzing data. Create a timeline of events.

■ **Develop data collection instruments**—There are many resources and templates available today to help. Most often you will not have to start from scratch. You may want to have a colleague review the assessments, surveys, and/or questionnaires to check for accuracy and ambiguity.

> FYI...
>
> **65 cents of every $1 spent on training is not focused on a business need.**

Steps in the Needs Analysis

1. Collect the Data

The first step is to collect the data. A challenge here is to determine the best way to collect data. Use more than one type of data collection. Be selective on who you include in the analysis. Common ways to collect data include:

■ **Observations**—Use a checklist of tasks and observe the person doing the job directly or watch a video of the person carrying out his or her job duties.

■ **Interviews**—Interview the person doing the job or the supervisor of the person doing the job.

■ **Focus Group**—Bring together a group of four to eight people from various jobs. Ask the group a series of questions or facilitate a discussion around specific topics.

■ **Surveys**—Write a series of questions on a form and send it to a targeted group of employees with a request of a response in a specific period of time.

Data Collection Methods

Method	Type
Observations	qualitative
Interviews	qualitative
Focus Groups	qualitative
Surveys	quantitative
Performance Data	quantitative

■ **Performance Data Analysis**—Examine reports and customer feedback to identify trends and patterns.

Each data collection method serves a specific purpose. Each type is either **qualitative,** based on perceptions, opinions, etc., of people, or more **quantitative**, which is based on facts and statistics rather than feeling or opinion. Understanding the difference is significant in the final analysis. Typically quantitative analysis carries more weight than qualitative. Each method of data collection can be both qualitative and quantitative.

At this point, you may also want to **benchmark** other companies in your industry to see what they are doing. Finally, you will want to review your company initiatives and organizational challenges that drive many company needs. Reviewing these initiatives and challenges should provide you with insight as you begin step 2.

> **TRAINER TERMS**
>
> **Benchmarking –**
> A practice of researching what other companies are doing with or about a particular problem in the industry

2. Analyze the Data

The next step is to analyze the data. In this step you need to compile all the information you have collected. You are looking to identify trends, problems, and opportunities. Make sure you have all your information before you begin. Making assumptions before you have all the information can cause you to miss critical data. Here are some things to look for when analyzing the data in a needs analysis:

■ **Problems or deficits**—Are there problems in the organization which can be solved by training?

■ **Change**—Is training needed to deal with changes in the workplace, new processes and equipment, competition, or staffing changes?

■ **Opportunities**—Is this an opportunity to take advantage of new technologies or new methods?

■ **Strengths**—What are we doing right? How can we use strengths in the organization to improve?

■ **Required Training**—Is training being required by management or the government? Are there internal or external forces dictating that training will take place?

■ **The People**—Who needs training? How much do they know about this area? How will they communicate? How do they learn best?

■ **The Organization**—Does management support the training? Is training valued in the organization?

■ **The Job**—What will the end result of training be back on the job? What is involved in doing the job? Where are the gaps in current skills vs. desired skills? How can participants take the training back and apply it to their work?

■ **Training Content**—What content needs to be covered in the training? Who are the experts who can help you develop the training? Who will deliver the training?

■ **Is Training the Right Solution?**—Will training be effective, or are there better ways to solve gaps?

■ **The Cost–** Calculate the Return on Investment (ROI). Are the end results worth the investment in developing and delivering training?

3. Prioritize the Gaps or Needs

The next step is to prioritize the gaps or needs. Once the data has been gathered and put in order, you can start looking at ways to satisfy the needs in the analysis. Part of this process is to prioritize the importance of the issues that have emerged. If you are having trouble prioritizing the issues, consider the following questions (parts excerpted from the U.S. Army, Civilian Training Model):

■ Do they deal with the organization's mission, goals, and objectives?

■ Do they impact organizational performance?

■ Do they involve short- and long-term skill requirements?

■ Do they impact the development of career paths?

■ Do they focus on key skill area requirements?

■ Do they consider individual needs in terms of organizational goals?

■ Do they involve the development of employees in career paths?

■ Are they significantly impacting the organization negatively?

■ Are there issues that need to be reviewed immediately?

4. Develop the Plan

The final step is to develop a plan of action. Now that the analysis is complete, you should have a clear idea of what is and is not a training issue. Based on the outcomes, you can put together a plan for resolution. The rest of this chapter will focus on the following elements of the training plan:

- **Decide on the storyline**, based on the results of your needs analysis.

- **Create measurable goals**. In other words, ask yourself: "What do I want to achieve?"

- **Write measurable learning objectives**. Ask yourself: "How will I achieve the goals?"

- **Set the standards for the performance.** Set the behaviors you expect your audience to be able to exhibit to accomplish the learning objectives.

- **Determine what tools you will use to measure the effectiveness of the class.**

DECIDING ON THE STORYLINE

As with any great performance, training begins with a great storyline. It begins with selecting a topic that fulfills an audience need. This topic must be specific, focused, and appropriate for that audience. Once the storyline is determined, it is then woven into a training script that provides useful, relevant information in an interesting, entertaining way. By the time you have finished your needs analysis, you should know what training is needed.

Trainers who do not have a clear vision of what the topic is will be less effective in satisfying the needs of their audience. Determine a topic and be very clear about the exact points you are trying to convey.

CREATING MEASURABLE GOALS

Creating goals begins with your review of the needs analysis. You must first answer the question—"What do I want to achieve?" **Goals** are used to set direction and frame your activities. A goal statement must be clear and concise. The goals for your training are considered to be the "what" of your achievements. After you write the goals, look at the company's mission, vision, business goals and key initiatives to make sure your training goals fit within them.

Example training goal statements:
- To orient all new employees to company operations and policies
- To train each line cook to the standard operation procedures of food item preparation
- To improve the delivery of service to all guests.

WRITING MEASURABLE LEARNING OBJECTIVES

The building blocks for well-designed training are the measurable objectives. If "what" is the goal, then "how" are the objectives. Review the original reasons, the needs analysis, for why the training is being developed. These reasons will drive the learning objectives.

With the overall goals of the company in mind and a clear understanding of why the topic was chosen, you can now write learning objectives for the training performance. They should be specific, clear, and measurable. Always include:

- **What you want your audience to learn.**
  - What skills should they be able to exhibit?
  - What knowledge will they be tested on?
  - What attitudes or perspectives should shift?
- **How you will test knowledge, competency, or compliance.**
  - What types of written testing will you administer?
  - What type of demonstrable skills assessments will you use?
  - What other measurements can you incorporate?
- **How you will determine the training was successful.**

- How will you determine how well the audience member is able to perform the new skill on the job?
- What business goals were you able to positively impact through the training?

An Example... Putting the Pieces Together

The Business Goal:

The Service Corp. has a goal this year to increase its customer service rating by 10%.

The Issue:

Careful analysis showed the greatest area for improvement is the reduction of catalogue order errors. You were asked to design a training class.

The Needs Analysis:

Determine what the employees needed to learn in order to reduce the number of errors. Further investigation showed many of the employees didn't know how to fill out the order form correctly. You decided the first training performance would be: How to correctly take an order and complete the accompanying form.

- What do you want the audience to learn?
  - Why the form should be used
  - When the form should be used
  - With whom the form should be used
  - How to accurately fill out the form
  - What items should not be included on the form
  - What the appropriate procedure is for processing the form after it is completed.
- How will you test their knowledge?
  - Provide them with a case study where a customer has called in an order. Include specific information in the case so the audience could complete the form.
  - Have them read the case study and complete the form.
  - Review their forms for accuracy.

(continued)

An Example... Putting the Pieces Together (continued)

- How will you determine if the training was successful?

  - Prior to the training performance, set up an agreement with the audience members' supervisors/managers to review forms, checking for completeness, accuracy, errors, etc.

  - In previous research, it was determined that correctly taken orders will drive up positive ratings for customer service. Based on this, the goal is 100% compliance in the use of the standardized form by all employees.

The Measurable Learning Objectives:

The learning objectives written for the class included:

- Every employee should be able to accurately (no mistakes) fill out an order form by the end of the class

- Every employee should be able to take an order from a customer using the appropriate form on the job.

Keep your objectives measurable by time, money, resources, and the individual.

SET THE STANDARDS OF PERFORMANCE

Setting the standards of performance helps clarify exactly what is expected in each objective. The **standards of performance** lists the behaviors needed to successfully accomplish the learning objectives. To develop the standards of performance, determine what specific actions, steps, skills, knowledge, and attitude need to be in place to accomplish the learning objectives. Keep in mind that the more detailed the specific actions are, the easier it will be to measure success.

An Example... Standards of Performance

Back to our previous example of the Service Corp. and the training performance: How to correctly take an order and complete the accompanying form.

In the previous example, the objectives included:

■ Every employee should be able to accurately (no mistakes) fill out an order form by the end of the class

■ Every employee should be able to take an order from a customer using the appropriate form back on the job.

Setting the Standards of Performance:

Determine what the employees would need to know in order to meet the learning objectives. The "**Best Practices**," written by the company, listed the following requirements:

TRAINER TERMS

Best Practice -
is a term used to refer to procedures or practices written by individuals in an organization, outlining the "best" way to do something

■ Employee answers the phone with a friendly greeting, using the standard script

■ Employee must be able to utilize the computer to accurately complete the order form

■ Employee needs to be able to look up catalogue numbers on the computer or in the master catalogue by item number

■ Employee needs to be able to total up the form, including cost of items, taxes, and shipping/delivery without errors

■ Employee needs to be able to verify the order with the customer.

These are the standards of performance. Based on all the information gathered, the rest of the script can be developed. These standards of performance will be the key topic areas for the script.

MEASUREMENT REQUIRES A PLAN

The focus of the training performance now turns to measurement. How are you going to measure the effectiveness of the class? This measurement is more than just asking the audience if they enjoyed the training performance. It is testing the learner for comprehension. The goal is to determine the measurement techniques that need to be incorporated into the script. These measurement techniques will only test the knowledge gained in the training performance, not necessarily how it will be applied or how well it has been applied.

For Example...

In the previous example, the objectives included:

■ Every employee should be able to accurately (no mistakes) fill out an order form by the end of the class

■ Every employee should be able to take an order from a customer using the appropriate form.

If we now consider these objectives, the measurement could include:

Objective 1. Role play an interaction with each trainee. The trainer plays a customer giving an order and the trainee takes the order using the form. Grade the forms for accuracy. The measurement: a minimum of 100% accuracy would be required for passing. (Anyone receiving lower than 100% would need to review errors and repeat the role-play process again.)

Objective 2. Have the training supervisor use an observation checklist in the workplace. This checklist would:

■ Include all the behaviors the employee should be practicing consistently.

■ Be used to rate the employee performing all the tasks.

Use the results of the observation checklist as a review with the employee.

Often trainers do not worry about evaluating the training until after it is over. The key is to start thinking about measurement at the inception of the process and carry it throughout the development of the entire training.

Types of Measurement

Measurement tools are used to determine how well a new skill has been learned. Measurement tools can be formal or informal. Depending on what you are trying to measure, some will be more quantitative, and others will be more qualitative. Measurement tools are a critical part of the training performance and should be as consistent and equitable as possible. Some types of measurement conducted during training include:

- **Skill or Performance Checks**—Performance checks are simple questions or mini-demonstrations asked of a learner after a skill or concept is taught. They are a great way to have your audience member check a skill before moving onto the next topic.

For Example...

You are teaching a class on behavioral interviewing. You just completed a 15-minute mini-lecture on writing behavioral interview questions. Now have the audience complete a skill check by having them write one behavioral question. Review their work by reading them aloud.

TRAINER TERMS

Performance Checks –
term used to refer to mini-quizzes, opportunities to model new behavior, to show that what was learned is incorporated throughout the training class, and to check whether the audience members are learning the content

- **Written Tests**—Written tests can include true/false statements, multiple-choice questions, fill-in-the-blank questions, or essay questions. Written tests are good tools for testing technical information that needs to be memorized.

For Example...

You have just finished a training performance on how to build a widget. You have the audience complete a fill-in-the-blank test highlighting the steps and tools needed to build the widget.

- **Demonstrable Assessments**—This is a skill test where the trainer watches the audience member demonstrate the new skill. It typically uses some type of checklist or set of criteria as a measurement tool.

For Example...

You have been conducting training performances in the kitchen. You have just completed a session on making a soup stock. Now you have your audience members collect ingredients and make their own soup stock. Using a step-by-step checklist, observe them in the process of making soup stock. The checklist helps you note any steps they miss in the process.

- **Videotaping**—Videotaping a trainee while he or she is demonstrating a specific skill is another great way of evaluating performance. The benefit of this tool is the ability to very accurately monitor behavior. An added bonus is the opportunity for the trainee and trainer to sit together and view the videotape. Collectively, the two can discuss and analyze what they are watching. Often the trainee is more critical than the trainer on evaluating his or her performance or behavior. Have a "score" sheet or grade sheet developed for measuring the activity.

For Example...

You have just completed a training performance on how to conduct a sales call to potential new clients. Put the audience into pairs and ask them to role play a sales call. As they conduct the role play, you videotape the interaction. Once the interaction is complete, review the tape together. Through your discussion, you can identify areas for improvement. You can also recognize a job well done!

- **Role-Play Exercises**—Role-play exercises are a great way for the trainer to assess how audience members will use the new information or how they will perform in a given situation before they have to do it on the job. Role-play exercises are also a great way for people to "act out" real-life scenarios and practice behaviors before having to do them "live."

For Example...

You have just completed a training performance for the tellers at the JCRiches Bank. The training was on how to greet customers and how to interact with them during a banking transaction. The session included proper greeting techniques, body language, facial expressions, and the standard "scripting" they should use. Once the training was completed, you had the audience break into pairs to conduct a role play. One member played the role of a customer while the other member played the role of the teller. During the role play, they were required to use all the things they had learned. Once they completed the initial role play, the pairs switched roles. Throughout the exercise, you observed the interactions, noting any problems, challenges, and great performances. You watched each pair to see that each audience member executed the new techniques properly and give the performers a chance to critique their own performance.

Some audience members may feel uncomfortable with role-play activity. It is important to recognize reluctance. Do not force someone who is not comfortable to take part. In these instances, develop an alternative way of measuring knowledge.

■ **Case Studies**—Case studies can be very simple or extremely complex. A case study is used to simulate a situation and have the audience take a predetermined action or answer questions. A training performance facilitator should assess analytical skills and knowledge through the audience action or response to the questions.

You have just completed a training performance on conflict management for the managers at the hotel you work for. Once the training was completed you grouped the managers into teams of four and gave them a case study. It described a scenario where several employees were having a heated discussion over a work-related issue. Based on the information they have just learned in the training performance, you require them to analyze the situation. You ask them to identify the issues in the case and determine how they would resolve the issues. Once the groups completed the discussion, you had them present their results to the rest of the audience members. Through the presentations, you were able to see how well the managers understood the basics of conflict management and if they were able to apply them.

■ **On-line Quizzes**—There are many ways to use technology as a measurement tool. There are new ways being developed every day. One of the more common ways is through on-line quizzes. Numerous software developers have created software to help you develop on-line quizzes or tests.

For Example...

You provided a group of new managers with an "individual development" training program. The program was divided into 16 specific modules or topic areas. You required them to go to their department's computer and log on to the company's intranet site after the completion of each training module. This intranet site hosted quizzes for every module. Audience members were required to access the appropriate on-line quiz, complete the quiz, and send it to you (via E-mail) for review.

FYI...

On-line quizzes could be on a computer disk or CD that is put into the computer. They can also be on-line via an Internet or intranet if your company has this technology.

■ **Simulation Exercises**—A simulation is a game that attempts to accurately recreate a particular situation, on a large or small scale. An example of large scale would be controlling a city, whereas small scale would be managing a hospital. Simulations can also provide a great way to evaluate and measure audience performance and knowledge.

For Example...

You work for a very large restaurant and bakery. You are asked by the owner to conduct a class on how to reduce operating costs for the business. The first part of the training performance provided information, processes, tools, etc., to audience members. The second part of the training performance was practice using a simulation game. The game was designed to have teams compete with each other. As the teams played the simulation, they needed to employ the strategies taught earlier in the performance. The team with the best results at the end of the competition won. Through this process, you were able to assess each team member's ability to grasp the concepts and apply them.

Training Performance Measurement Tools

Type of measurement	What is it used for?	When is it used?	Who administers it?
Skill or Performance Checks	Check for comprehension throughout the training process	After completing each module	Instructor or audience member
Written Tests	Test factual knowledge	Any time throughout training	Instructor
Demonstrable Assessments	Show ability to perform task	Any time throughout training	Instructor
Checklists	Show understanding of the various job tasks	Back in the work environment	Instructor or manager
Role-Play Exercises	Show thought process or ability to perform task in given situations	Any time throughout training	Instructor
Videotaped Practice Sessions	Self-evaluation through self-observation	Any time throughout training	Instructor or others
Case Studies	Show reactions to real-life situations	Any time throughout training	Instructor
On-Line Quizzes	Test factual knowledge	Any time throughout training	Learner through technology
Simulation Exercises	Show reactions in real-life situations	Any time throughout training	Instructor

Pre- and Post-Test Measures

When planning for measurement, be sure to think through the pre- and post-test measures. You will want to be able to make strong statements about the impact of your training. Additionally, be fully prepared to test the learner after he or she has returned to his or her job assignment. This will allow you to evaluate the lasting effects of the training.

The evaluation you do during a session can help you revise your training while in process—this is known as **formative evaluation**. Evaluation done at the end of training is known as **summative evaluation** and focuses on what the learner knows or demonstrates in skills.

Write It or Buy It

Technology isn't the only thing that could cost significant amounts of money. Off-the-shelf training, or customized training, can be purchased as well. And as in business, when purchasing high cost or capital assets, it is important to do your homework. Off-the-shelf or pre-written training programs are available in many formats for just about any situation. Many of these are very good. Many also have a significant price tag. There are hundreds of designers and developers prepared to customize a training program for any occasion. Before purchasing these, consider the following:

1. What type of support is provided?
2. What percentage of their off-the-shelf program is customizable?
3. What are the copyright issues regarding use of the program?
4. What is the policy for updates to the program?
5. Is the fee a one-time fee, a per use/attendee fee, or is there a renewal fee?
6. Are the evaluation methods suited to your needs?

Do not get caught up in the "sell." Make sure the item or program you are purchasing is the one you think you are purchasing.

TRADITIONAL INSTRUCTIONAL DESIGN

For many years, the standard process for identifying and developing training needs has been through a **traditional instructional design** (TID) approach. This method provides the basic structure for designing and developing effective training. It is a step-by-step process, stressing thoroughness and effectiveness

Traditional Instructional Design (TID)– a step-by-step process for identifying and developing training

and involves much time to evaluate patterns, jobs, and processes. The focus of TID is to make employees more efficient in their work environments.

The challenges with using TID in today's business climate is that the very structured processes involved take too long. Eight- to twelve-month development times are not uncommon in TID. Most of today's trainers do not have the luxury of the time and money required to use this type of model. By the time training would be ready for delivery, it would no longer be needed! It is important, however, to understand the basic elements of the model, as it does provide the roots of today's process, and its principles still drive much of today's training.

> FYI...
>
> We are typically developing new training products in two, sometimes three months. That's the turnaround time from the initial needs analysis to rolling the training program out.
>
> *William Knapp Sr., Manager of Global Virtual Learning Infrastructure, Deloitte Consulting.*

Sample Traditional Instructional Design Model

Step 1. The Job Analysis

The primary purpose of a job analysis is to study people in an organization who are excellent in their jobs. The goal is to watch how the best performer does his or her job and use that method as a standard for performance. In turn, these practices become the best practices for training. In this step you are trying to find out:

- What tools they use
- What steps they take
- What information or level of education they need to excel in the job.

Step 2. Develop Learning Objectives

Conduct an analysis of the people who will fill the jobs. Here the trainer is looking at the **gap** between what is required to be successful and the skill base of the employees doing the job. The learning objectives are designed to close the gap between the two.

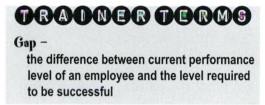

TRAINER TERMS

Gap –
the difference between current performance level of an employee and the level required to be successful

Step 3. Design Training Accordingly

Having determined the needs and learning objectives, the next step is to design training to accomplish the objectives. Keys to keep in mind in this phase include:

- What types of training to use
- The length of the training
- Any special considerations regarding the training (i.e., who is delivering the training, when employees will receive it).

Step 4. Develop and Pilot Test the Training

Once the training has been written, you now have to test it. Pilot testing is done by setting up a class and conducting a pilot training session. The trainees in the pilot class should mirror the intended target population as closely as possible. The objective is to test the materials, design, and training methods. An imperative portion of this phase is substantial audience feedback. Feedback from supervisors, managers, and other stakeholders are also valuable.

FYI...

Pilot classes that include key stakeholders either as participants or as observers provide crucial feedback from a perspective different from target population of the class.

Step 5. Access the Training

Now that the pilot test is complete and the feedback is in, it is time to take an honest look at the training module.

- Did it accomplish the objectives?
- Did it fit within the time frame allotted?
- Did the audience get involved?
- Did the audience learn what it was supposed to learn?
- What did the audience find most effective? Least effective?
- Most important, what changes need to be made?

Step 6. Make the Changes

Make the changes recommended in Step 5. Conduct the training for the intended audiences. It is important to measure your results continuously. Do not assume once the training design is done, it's written in stone! You may have to revise and repeat the process. Keep an ongoing audit of your audience.

Frequently, trainers skip audience feedback or disregard it if the feedback is inconsistent with their own opinions. Remember, you are designing the class for the audience, not for yourself!

Traditional instructional design provides the basic structure for today's model of training. We have just adapted the model for the speed of today's business.

Skill Builders

1. Describe the steps of needs analysis to be done before undertaking a training project.

2. How do you select an appropriate training performance measurement tool?

3. List techniques for securing effective feedback from key stakeholders regarding potential training initiatives.

4. Describe the difference between a symptom and a root cause.

5. Analyze the types of measurement; include pros and cons for each.

Chapter 3

YOU AS THE ACTOR

Every time you teach poorly, you are creating a future problem. Every time you teach well, you are solving a future problem. — UCLA Office of Instructional Development

IN THIS CHAPTER:

- **Role of the Actor**
- **Communicating with Your Audience**
- **Behaviors that Impact Learning**
- **Know Your Material**
- **Skill Builders**

Role of the Actor

When you go to a brilliant theatrical performance or watch an outstanding movie, what sets it apart from other less engaging ones? The ability of the actor to connect with the audience, to move or engage the audience in a very special way takes the performance from mediocre to memorable. In the same spirit, the trainer or "actor" in a training performance has a direct impact on whether people learn, what they learn, and how much they learn. A good actor can even take a flawed script and make it a successful performance by his or her knowledge, presence, and ability to communicate with the audience. The actor impacts the audience with his or her:

- Words
- Actions
- Attitude
- Knowledge.

Communicating with Your Audience

The most important skill effective actors need to possess is the art of communication. Communication is more than just talking; it's both the words you choose (verbal communication) and an understanding of how you use your voice and body to enhance your message in a variety of ways (nonverbal communication). Listening is another critical skill to connecting with your audience. Concentrate on these areas when communicating with your audience:

- Choose your words carefully. Consider your audience's educational level, background, and primary language
- Focus on how you will deliver your lines, including your volume, enunciation, speed, inflection, and use of fillers.
- Use proper vocabulary. Watch repetition and the use of jargon, slang, and profanity in your performance.
- Consider your non-verbals, including gestures and facial expressions. Are they distracting or offensive to particular members of your audience?

■ Dress for success. Keep in mind that how you dress is a powerful form of communication.

Your Words

The primary way of delivering information is by what you say. The words you use affect the message the audience receives. When you know who your audience is and what they want from the training, you can deliver better training. Having a strong, well written script will help you. To help choose the right words, consider the:

■ Educational level of your audience

■ Primary language of your audience

■ Background of your audience.

Choosing words and terms that are difficult to understand, words that are inappropriate, or words that offend can negatively impact the learning experience.

Educational Level of Your Audience

Understand the educational level of your audience. Using complicated words with an audience comprised of members who have lower educational levels will affect their ability to understand what you say. If you are using words that are too simple and mundane with an audience comprised of executives or scholars, you may bore them. Effective communication means first understanding who your audience is and then choosing words they can understand.

The Primary Language of Your Audience

Consider the diversity of your audience when choosing words to communicate your message. Use simpler words if your audience's primary language is not English. Using basic words and eliminating slang will improve your communication. Many words can have different meanings for different people. Using these words can confuse people and block their ability to understand your message.

> ### An Example...
> You are a trainer in a hotel. You're doing a training on the different types of hotels in the United States. You have a diverse audience of international interns. You begin your presentation with a discussion on
>
> **(continued)**

An Example... (continued)

"mom and pop" motels. As you begin the discussion, you notice audience members are looking very confused. Someone asks you what their mother and Coca-Cola have to do with running a motel! You explain the term "mom and pop" is a slang term referring to small businesses owned and operated by one individual.

The Background of Your Audience

Every industry has words and acronyms specific only to that industry or company. Before you use these acronyms in your performance, it is important to define them for the audience. Don't assume they know them or they can figure them out on their own. By defining terms and acronyms for your audience, it helps clarify the information and gives them a sense of belonging.

An Example...

You are showing a group of restaurant employees a new booklet on food sanitation from the NRA. Someone asks why the National Rifle Association has a food book. You laugh and tell them it's from the National Restaurant Association. Don't assume people know what the initials mean.

When working in an industry, people often use acronyms without thinking about it. When using acronyms or words specific to your company or industry during your training performance, stop and explain what they mean.

Delivering Your Lines

In the theater, the actor plays a key role in the effectiveness of a performance. How you use your voice can make the difference in whether the audience listens to you or not. Imagine an actor speaking so softly and quickly you have to struggle to listen and keep up. Now imagine an actor who projects his voice and uses dramatic pauses. Which would you rather listen to? Take these same techniques and apply them to your training performance. Some of these techniques include:

- Use a volume that is comfortable, but one that can be heard by all.

- Use a microphone if you are working with a very large group. If the audience members in the back have to struggle to hear, they will disengage from the performance.

> **FYI . . .**
>
> **Speak as if you are speaking to the person in the back row of the performance. By doing this, you will always be loud enough for all the audience members to hear.**

- Enunciate words, don't mumble or fall off at the end of sentences.

- Speak slowly enough for everyone to understand.

- Use voice inflection to impact what you are saying. (A monotone voice puts an audience to sleep faster than anything else!)

- Avoid using filler words such as "uumms," "uuuhhhs," "like," and "you knows." These fillers take away from the message and annoy the audience.

Actors who are very nervous tend to use more fillers than those who are calm and relaxed. Prepare, rehearse, and use techniques to minimize the "jitters"!

Have a Good Vocabulary

Using proper vocabulary can make or break a performance. Know your audience and cater your language choices to them.

- Use language that's appropriate for your audience.

- Avoid repeating words or phrases too often. This can turn an audience off.

- Too much jargon or slang will also lose your audience.

- Don't use profanity during a performance.

Do you want to improve your performance? Videotape one of your training sessions and watch the video. Seeing yourself on video can be traumatic! You start finding fault with everything. Do not be too tough on yourself. Look at your performance from the audience's eyes. Take notes on what you did well and where you would like to improve. During your critique, make sure you identify at least five things you did well in addition to the things you are identifying for improvement.

Your Actions

Nonverbal communication plays a tremendous role in performance. Think back to a great performance you saw. How did the actors use their bodies to convey their message or tell their story? The same effective techniques the actor uses in a theatrical performance work in a training performance. We are a visual society and, as such, we tend to give more credit to what we see than what we hear!

Nonverbal communication is communication without words. The basics of nonverbal communication include:

- Body movement
- Facial expressions
- Gestures
- Inflection
- Eye contact.

TRAINER TERMS

Nonverbal communication–
   communication without words
Kinesics –
   the study of bodily movements

Body Movement

Kinesics, the study of body movement, is a large part of nonverbal communication. How you stand, move, or use your body can make a significant impact on how your message is received. It can also drive the energy in the room. If you are standing straight, and you are facing the audience, your audience will reflect the same posture. If you are slouching and you have your arms crossed in front of you with your hands wrapped around your elbows, people assume you are angry or disagree with what they are saying. Your audience will be less likely to respond to you and what you say.

Gestures

Gestures, any body movements, can take the place of words or enhance the words you are saying. Gestures often help clarify or reinforce what is being said to the listener. Greet your audience members in the morning as they are arriving by shaking everyone's hand as you welcome them, rather than just saying good morning. By doing this, the audience members feel you are taking

FYI...

The larger the number of audience members, the greater the chance for misunderstanding. Using your nonverbal actions correctly can help your audience understand your message.

the time to not only welcome them individually, but are sincerely interested in their learning. It sets a good tone to begin the class.

Facial Expressions and Eye Contact

Your facial expressions show the audience your level of sincerity, excitement, and enthusiasm for the topic. If you are bored with the training topic and your face shows it, your audience is likely to be bored as well. Smiling is one of the best things you can do to convey your interest in the material.

What Your Face May Be Telling Someone...

I am happy. *I am serious.* *I am kidding.* *I am surprised.*

I am paying attention to you. *I don't like what you're saying.* *I don't believe that.* *That is funny.*

Eye contact is the single most significant part of facial expressions. Using direct eye contact can move an audience to action. Lack of eye contact could convey you are not being truthful or you don't believe what you are saying. If an audience member is asking a question and you are looking around instead of at him or her, he or she may feel as if you are not paying attention or are not interested. They may feel they are an interruption to you, and your audience may stop asking questions.

> FYI...
> Direct eye contact does not mean nonstop staring at someone. It means regularly looking into the audience's eyes (not past them).

Total Body Movement

To get the maximum effect during a performance, your body, voice, and actions should match. Your gestures, voice, and words should be saying the same thing. If you are trying to convey something very serious, your facial expressions should be serious, your gestures calm, and your voice lower. When your nonverbal communication is consistent with your verbal message, you are more believable to your audience.

Appearance

Just as the actor's costume plays a significant role in an effective performance, so does the trainer's appearance in the training performance. People make decisions, form opinions, and judge the abilities of someone based on how he or she looks. Grooming, hygiene standards, and your clothing are all a part of the "costume," impacting your credibility. Good appearance includes:

- **Hygiene**—For most people, being clean is a way of life. Bathing, washing your hair, and generally practicing sound sanitary practices are all a part of hygiene.

- **Grooming Standards**—Grooming includes your clothes, shoes, accessories, etc. Your audience members will follow your lead. The impression you present is the standard they will practice.

Which one looks like the trainer?

■ **Clothing**—Your clothes should be clean, neat, and pressed to convey a professional appearance. Dress as well as the best-dressed person in the audience. Be sure to follow your company policies or dress code. Even if you are giving a presentation in a casual environment, you should look neat and clean.

Your Energy Level

If you use up all your energy in the early part of the training performance, you won't be able to finish the way you want. As you lose energy, so will your audience. There are certain times during the day when everyone's energy dips. Recognizing when these occur and having a strategy in place to combat them will enhance the training performance.

Listening to Your Audience

Listening is often the most important part of communication. How we listen to our audience and interpret their feedback may be the difference between getting our message across and missing the mark. Listening involves more than just using our ears. Watching the audience's body movements and facial expressions can communicate important information back to you. You can tell if the audience:

■ Is frustrated

■ Has a question

■ Is disagreeing with what is being said

■ Understands the information being delivered.

To be a better listener and to fully understand the audience member speaking in your performance:

■ **Mentally rephrase** what they are saying as they are communicating with you.

■ **Empathize**. There are times when the audience member is coming from a different perspective from yours. Try to understand it.

■ **Don't assume** you know what the audience members are saying. Restate what they have said for clarity.

■ **Don't evaluate.** When we judge or disapprove of what the audience members are saying, we close the door to really hearing them.

Effective actors watch to see if the audience's words are consistent with their body language and facial expression. Look for nodding heads and eye contact from the audience. If everyone is sitting with a glazed expression on their faces, you may need to change your delivery, use an energizing class activity, or review the topic for clarity.

Remember, listening involves:

- Listening with your eyes and your ears. Watch nonverbal communication as well as listening to what is being said.
- Asking open-ended questions for clarification.
- Giving the audience time to answer a question before rephrasing or repeating what you asked.
- Listening for both the stated facts and the unstated emotions in the answer to a question to get all the information that is being communicated.

Listening Means Asking Questions

Effective listening includes asking questions. They may be questions of clarification, questions to get more information, or questions to encourage more discussion. Understanding the way you ask questions can determine the kind of answers you receive. During a performance, actors often ask the audience: "Do you understand?" to verify if the content being presented is understood. The audience will often say "yes" even when they don't understand. They don't want to say "no" because they don't want to appear slow or unsure. If you really want to see if your audience understands the information, ask open-ended questions that require them to answer, explain, describe, or summarize.

An Example...

Good Question:
    "Give me an example of when you need to clean your work area."

Bad Question:
    "Do you need to clean your work area at the end of your shift?"

Waiting for the Answer

Once you have asked a question, pause and wait for the answer. This is a difficult practice for most people. Our tendency is to immediately ask another question. Some people take longer to plan their answer than do others. Once they do answer, listen to the complete answer. Many trainers hear the first part of the answer, and if it sounds familiar, they immediately assume what the rest of the answer is without really listening to the full response. It takes practice to be able to completely listen to what someone says.

Trainers often start generalizing and providing answers before the audience member finishes asking the question. Be sure to listen to the whole question before replying.

Listen for Fact & Emotion

When listening to your audience, listen for both the facts being stated and the emotions in the message. If you only listen to the facts, you are missing part of the information. When you listen for the emotion in their voices and actions, you can get a clearer picture of what they are really saying. Emotions can play a significant role in the learning process.

An Example...

You ask an audience member to explain the steps to proper hand washing. He gives you the correct steps, but his voice and actions indicate he doesn't plan on following them in the workplace. This would be a good time to stop and explain the importance of following the procedure. You can effect change in the attitude of the audience if you take advantage of your opportunities.

BEHAVIORS THAT IMPACT LEARNING

In addition to effective communication, there are several other behaviors that play a significant role in how well your audience learns. As the actor in the training performance, you become a role model to the audience. To be a good role model, there are some common behaviors you should follow:

■ **Be Consistent**—The audience is watching what you do and comparing your actions to your words. If what you say doesn't match what you do, they will question your integrity, or stop listening to you altogether.

■ **Respect**—Treat your audience in a manner that is polite, unbiased, and considerate. If your audience feels respected by you, they will be more open to

An Example...

You are facilitating a training performance on conflict management. One of the lessons you are trying to convey is to never correct an employee in front of other people because it hurts their dignity. You then reprimand or correct an audience member in front of everyone during the training performance. The audience sees your action was not consistent with what you said. They question your credibility. What should they listen to, what you said or what you did?

asking questions, sharing their thoughts and ideas, and taking an active role in the performance.

■ **Act Professionally**—Be professional both on and off stage. Some keys to being professional include:

■ Treat everyone with respect

■ Be sincere

■ Treat everyone with dignity and equality

■ Be physically and mentally prepared for the performance

■ Do what you say you are going to do and follow through with commitments. This plays a larger part in building credibility with your audience.

■ Celebrate success. When an audience member does a great job, recognize his or her contribution.

■ **Practice good etiquette**—Manners, attitude and behavior in a training performance can make a significant impact on its effectiveness. Some specific behaviors include:

■ Say please and thank you. For example, say: "Would everyone please get into groups of four?" rather than "Get into groups of four!"

■ Respect your audience.

Trainer "No-Nos"

There will be times when someone in the audience will frustrate or annoy you. Be sure to treat him or her the same way as you would everyone else. A professional will provide the greatest opportunities to get everyone involved and ready to learn. The more everyone feels respected, the more interested they will be in the training performance. If there is one audience member annoying the rest of the audience, deal with him or her immediately. If you don't deal with it, your audience will become frustrated and tune out. Handle the situation in a professional manner by pulling him or her aside during a break and correcting his or her behavior.

> **FYI . . .**
> People listen with their eyes 93% of the time (watching what you do, and how you act) and with their ears only 7% of the time (listening to the words you say)!

There are some absolute "no-nos" or behaviors you should never do in the training environment:

- Never use vulgar language
- Never make fun of any trainee
- Never make inappropriate or sexist remarks
- Never discriminate against anyone for any reason
- Never talk about one trainee to another trainee.

KNOW YOUR MATERIAL

As a trainer, you need to be confident and have full knowledge about your topic. Showing experience and self-confidence to your audience gives them confidence in you. If they feel you know your topic and you are confident, they will listen. Be prepared and study your material before you get to the performance. Proper preparation includes:

- Observing others training on the same material
- Knowing the script and the flow of your training
- Anticipating audience questions
- Talking with the training developer if you have questions

■ Knowing when to ask for help from others.

Knowing your material can make you feel much more confident even if you are not an experienced trainer.

Arrogance vs. Self-Confidence

It is important to feel confident about the material you are presenting. Acting arrogantly, however, is unacceptable. Arrogance, or a "know-it-all attitude," causes students to stop listening. Arrogance also impedes your ability to listen to your audience. If no one is listening, the learning environment will be ineffective.

Answering Questions

A common mistake trainers make is trying to answer a question when they don't know the answer. If you don't know the answer, don't pretend you do. Tell your audience member you don't know but you'll find the answer. Then make sure you do find the answer and give it to the audience member who asked. Many audience members appreciate your willingness to admit you don't know everything. It can help build connections with the audience.

Pretending to know an answer to a question when you don't seriously damages your credibility with your audience. It's more important to know where to get the answers than to know all the answers!

SKILL BUILDERS

1.   How do you prepare for a training performance?

2.   How do you handle a question during a training performance you do not know the answer to?

3.   What strategies would you use to calm yourself before a training performance?

4.   Create a list of techniques you plan to employ to assist you in effectively listening to your audience.

Chapter 4

THE AUDIENCE

Personally, I am always ready to learn, although I do not always like being taught. — Winston Churchill

IN THIS CHAPTER:

- **Identify the Audience**
- **How People Learn**
- **Demographics**
- **Reference**
- **Skill Builders**

IDENTIFY THE AUDIENCE

When a playwright sets out to develop a storyline into a script, the first thing he or she does is identify the audience. Who will come to the performance? What age groups will be interested? What types of characters will they identify with? What props are needed on the set to keep their attention? Answers to these and other questions provide the playwright with critical information on how the story should be told.

When developing a storyline for training, asking these types of questions about your participants or audience will help ensure your success as well. Clearly identify your audience, and you can design the training session to better meet their needs. Training that fits the needs of the audience will create "sticky" training. Sticky training is training that is transferred back to the workplace. This type of training only happens when the training is well thought out, fun to learn, and relevant to the lives of the audience.

HOW PEOPLE LEARN

Before you can develop your script, you need to understand how people learn. It is more important to structure your training to the needs of the audience rather than following the teaching styles of the trainer.

Adult Learning Principles

It's important to understand that adults learn differently from children. Many studies have been done on adult learning. While these studies may vary somewhat, there are some common themes:

- Adult learners are "hands on." They need to be able to touch what they are learning. They need to experience it whenever possible. Get them involved in their own learning experience.

- Adult learners base what they are learning on previous experience. They use past experiences as a reference. They will look at the current training through the lenses of what they have already learned. This can sometimes cause difficulty when trying to show a completely different practice or new way of looking at something.

■ Adult learners expect that what they are being taught is relevant to what they are currently doing, what they want to do next, or how it could help them personally.

■ Adult learners will only learn when they want to learn.

■ Adult learners learn best when the training is entertaining and interesting.

■ No trainer can motivate a learner. The learner motivates his or herself.

■ Adult learners remember what they help discover themselves. Let the learner share in the discovery of solutions and new information.

■ Give adult learners the opportunity to pass on what they have learned to others.

■ Adult learners respond to recognition, encouragement, and approval.

An Example . . .

You are teaching a class on how to use your company's accounting program in the computer system. You put each audience member at a computer terminal. As you conduct the training you integrate opportunities for the audience to practice what they are being taught. If you try this training session with only a workbook, the training will be less effective because the audience can't experience the learning as you are teaching.

Getting "Buy-In" from the Learner

Another strategy for helping the audience learn is to help them see how "what" they are learning is tied to their work or personal goals. Showing them the **"WIIFM"** or the benefit of the training can help them "buy-in" to your performance. If people understand how "what" they are learning is going to benefit them, it becomes easier for them to listen and learn.

TRAINER TERMS

What's In It For Me? (WIIFM) -
is an acronym used to refer to the term "What's In It For Me." It is used when showing people the benefit of the activity or action being discussed.

Trainers assume the audience can always see the personal benefits of attending training. This is not always the case. Great trainers help their audience visualize how the training will help them accomplish a goal, increase their earning potential, or learn a new skill.

DEMOGRAPHICS

Demographics, the personal characteristics of an audience, is a key piece in both writing the script and in the delivery of the actual performance. Some of the most important components to look at in the audience are:

TRAINER TERMS

Demographics -
term used to refer to the statistical characteristics or composition of a particular group. It includes facts such as geographic origin, cultural background, age, gender, etc.

■ Cultural background

■ Experience level and position in the company

■ Generational differences.

Cultural Background

A classroom filled with people of varied cultural backgrounds can create a rich learning experience. An effective trainer quickly learns to draw experiences from various audience members into the discussion. When designing training for a culturally diverse audience, it is important to ask yourself the following questions:

■ Is English a second language for your audience?

   If it is, use a vocabulary that can be understood. You will also want to be careful not to use slang, jargon, or heavy pronoun usage.

- Have they lived in cultures that would cause them to not understand or be able to relate to practical examples used in the training?

  Those who may have grown up in another country may not understand using an example of something you experienced while growing up in America.

- Can everyone read and write English?

  Being able to speak and understand English does not automatically mean a person can read and write it. You may have to use more graphics and pictures to help the audience understand their training materials.

FYI . . .

Current studies suggest that between 30% and 40% of all future jobs not requiring an advanced education will be filled by immigrants and their children.

An Example...

You have been charged with rolling out the new benefits program for your company. You will be creating a benefits booklet, as well as conducting several classes to teach the line-level associates what their benefits are and how they can access them. Fifty percent of your audience speaks fluent Spanish and has English as their second language. You want to make sure they understand all the information. Translate the booklet into their language and have a translator in class to help you.

Experience Level and Position in Company

The experience level of your audience will dictate your vocabulary, the timing of your performance, and the level of detail you choose to incorporate into your performance. You will need to provide greater detailed information, a more comprehensive explanation, and add additional activities into performances with audiences that have little experience with your topic.

You may find yourself challenged with an audience that has a variety of experience levels. When this occurs, you may choose to pair less experienced members with more experienced members. This will allow for a greater transfer of knowledge between participants as well as from you.

The positions in the company your audience members hold will also affect your training performance. An audience full of executives will demand a shorter performance with fewer details and more specific information. An audience comprised of line-level employees may demand a longer performance with detailed information. Both groups will need activities; however you may need to be more creative in your delivery for executives.

Generational Differences

Generational differences play a significant role in how you write your script and design your performance. Different age or generational groups learn differently, using different methods. In today's workplace, there are four separate generations working together in the workplace and learning together in the classroom. In his book, *Generations at Work*, Ron Zemke describes a "generational phenomenon" currently being experienced in workplaces everywhere. He describes how each of the four generations has characteristics unique to that generation.[1]

Each of these generations has experienced common **defining moments** that have shaped their views, beliefs, perspectives, and behaviors. Because of their experiences, each group has a different learning style. This is not an attempt to stereotype or profile any

TRAINER TERMS

Defining Moments - a term used in Zemke's *"Generations At Work"* as the moments throughout a person's life that have made a significant impact on who that person is and how they think [1]

person or persons. Understanding who is in your audience can help you design training that is appropriate. **Keep in mind there will always be exceptions.** If your training will include people from different generations, you should include a variety of activities and learning moments to address the learning needs of all students.

Generations: Defining Moments and Learning Preferences

Generation	Born Between the Years of	Defining Moments	Learning Preferences
Veterans	1922-1943	■ The depression ■ World War II ■ The silver screen ■ New Deal ■ Golden age of radio ■ Families.	Respond to traditional classroom instruction with lectures given by topic experts. They prefer language that is logical and nonemotional. They prefer a more formal training environment.

Generations: Defining Moments and Learning Preferences (continued)

Generation	Born Between the Years of	Defining Moments	Learning Preferences
Baby Boomers	1943-1960	■ Vietnam ■ Television ■ Civil rights ■ Cold war ■ Women's liberation ■ Suburbia ■ Rock 'n' roll ■ The assassination of a president.	Respond well to many different training formats. They enjoy team building opportunities. They prefer a more casual environment and with more participative, interactive format and are not fond of role playing.
Generation X	1960-1980	■ Watergate ■ Single-parent homes ■ First latch key generation ■ MTV ■ AIDS ■ Fall of Berlin Wall.	This group is very comfortable with computer-based training. However, they also enjoy classroom training. They believe in practice and appreciate role playing.
Nexter's	1980 to Present	■ Born with technology ■ TV talk shows ■ Schoolyard violence ■ Oklahoma bombing.	Learn best in highly interactive environments. Extremely comfortable with technology. Work best on projects in teams.

The Point and Click Generation

In addition to Zemke's generational phenomenon, current research is showing just how much new technology is changing the way employees just entering the work force are beginning to learn. Often more comfortable with technology than with people, this new breed of worker processes information differently. Previous generations learned in a more linear fashion. Young people are using computers at very early ages. When using a computer, you have a menu of choices and can choose the order of learning by simply pointing to the choice and clicking on it. Consider the needs of the user and how they learn when developing your script, deciding on the types of activities, and delivering the performance.

REFERENCE

1.   Zemke, Ron. *Generations at Work*. AMACOM, New York. 2000.

SKILL BUILDERS

1.   List the key principles to adult learning.

2.   Create a list of WIIFMs (What's in it for me) you would look for in a training setting. Choose a specific training topic, for a specific industry, to be delivered in a short timeframe.

3.   Choose an organization you are familiar with. Create a profile of potential participants for a training class. The participant profile will be provided to another trainer who will be developing a training performance. The profile should include, but not be limited to, information on demographics, company culture, and experience levels of the trainees.

Chapter 5

DEVELOPING THE SCRIPT

PART 1: THE OUTLINE

Most people are more comfortable with old problems than with new solutions. — Anonymous

IN THIS CHAPTER:

- **The Script**
- **Brainstorming Your Content**
- **Organizing Your Information**
- **Creating an Outline**
- **Making the Training Schedule**
- **Types of Training**
- **Off the Shelf Training**
- **References**
- **Skill Builders**

THE SCRIPT

The heart of the performance, the **script**, is the story the actors bring to life for the audience. Having a great idea for a story is not enough. It is how the playwright develops each character or part of the story that determines how the audience will respond. This same thing applies when developing the script for your training performance. Each part of the training script needs to be developed in concert with all the other parts of the training script. You need to have:

■ Well-developed content, designed specifically for the audience

■ A performance that threads activities, creativity, and a learner-centered approach

■ Well-thought-out, well-organized creative participant materials

■ A way to measure effectiveness.

It's very difficult to deliver a great performance with a poor script. Even the best actor's performance skills are useless if the content is not relevant, appropriate, and well written.

Your script should include:

■ Goals

■ Measurable learning objectives

■ Standards of performance expected from your audience that support the learning objectives

■ Specific directions on how to deliver or perform the script

■ Tools used to measure success.

FYI...
Writing the script with a focus on quality, creativity, and content is the difference between mediocrity and meaningful.

Script writing can be overwhelming on your first attempt. To make the process easier, break it down into several steps. In this book, script development has been divided into three parts and is covered in three chapters:

- Chapter 5: determining the content of the performance (what materials to cover)

- Chapter 6: creating the elements of the performance (deciding how to present the information)

- Chapter 7: developing your props (creating your workbooks and visual materials).

At-a-Glance Guide to Script Writing

Part 1: Developing the Outline – Chapter 5	
Brainstorm Content, Review Research	■ Brainstorm information to include in the training ■ Refer to the needs analysis ■ Review the audience profile ■ Revisit your training goals.
Organize Content, Set Goals, and Create Measurable Learning Objectives	■ Organize content by topic area ■ Set the specific goals for the training performance based on the needs analysis ■ Write specific, clear, and measurable objectives that help to reach the goals.
Develop the Content Outline	■ Outline your general topics ■ Consult subject matter experts ■ Organize and prioritize your key points.
Write the Training Schedule	■ Determine length of the performance ■ Decide on the amount of time to spend on each key point ■ Integrate activities around low energy level times of day ■ Find the time for training.
Review Different Training Methods	■ Examine the different types of training and determine which delivery methods to use ■ Consider off the shelf products.

At-a-Glance Guide to Script Writing (continued)

Part 2: Elements of the Performance – Chapter 6

Develop Mini-lessons for Each Key Point Area	■ Use your outline as a template and begin to create small lesson chunks.
Decide How to Present the Information	■ Consider using visuals ■ Gather written materials ■ Use creative thinking methods and exercises ■ Schedule games and activities.
Engage the Learner	■ Use methods that make learning fun for the users ■ Use humor appropriately.
Include Measurement	■ Thread performance checks that measure learning throughout the training session ■ Utilize a variety of measurement tools.
Open and Close the Session	■ Plan session openings and closings ■ Incorporate ice breakers and set expectations ■ Close the session on a high note.

Part 3: Creating the Props – Chapter 7

Audience Script (Participant's Handbook)	■ Develop training workbooks ■ Develop handouts and materials for the audience.
Develop Audio/Visual Aids	■ Develop any overheads, presentations, graphics, flip charts, etc., needed.
Actor's Script (Facilitator's Guide)	■ Create notes for the actor to follow during the performance ■ Incorporate references to visuals, activities, written materials, breaks, exercises, etc.
Be Ethical	■ Give credit where credit is due.

Developing the Content Outline

By the time you get to this step and are ready to create your training program, you should have a good understanding of what you want to accomplish and how you will measure learner performance. In Chapter 2, *Why Do You Need Training?*, you learned how to do a needs analysis to decide what training was needed. You also learned how to write goals and measurable objectives, and the different ways to measure the abilities of the learner. Now you need to look at all this information and decide what to include in the training.

BRAINSTORMING YOUR CONTENT

Begin the script development by brainstorming a list of all the things you want to include in the session. Gather the following resources to help you identify your content:

■ Needs analysis
■ Standards of performance on the job
■ Training goals and objectives
■ Any research you conducted in developing your storyline
■ Content experts, supervisors or managers, or other trainers
■ Research on what other companies are doing in this area.

Creative Brainstorming Techniques

In script writing, the greatest challenge is often in where to start! Collecting and organizing the appropriate information in a way that is meaningful for the audience can be overwhelming. Creative brainstorming techniques can help you get past any mental blocks. Pick and choose from the following brainstorming techniques to find one that works for you. When one technique isn't working, try another!

Writing Down Every Idea (even the bad ones!)

Sometimes we are our own worst enemy when it comes to brainstorming. We come up with an idea, and before we even explore it, we decide it isn't any good and dismiss it. Write down all your ideas without critiquing them. There will be plenty of time for that later. It's been said the first three or four ideas you have on a topic are not the best ones. It's only after you have listed more than a few ideas that the better ideas start coming!

Storyboarding

One brainstorming technique is storyboarding. Storyboarding is a visual display used to help solve complex ideas or problems. All you need to storyboard are index cards, a pen, and a poster board or wall. Start by writing down your major topic headings on the board. Then brainstorm ideas about the major topics. Write your ideas on index cards and place them under the most logical major heading. This board or wall becomes an "idea landscape." Move the idea cards around as needed in order to develop the best possible story (or script).[1]

Creative Mind Mapping

Mind mapping is another brainstorming technique you may want to use. It's basically getting information down on paper in a way your mind can read it or in a way that "maps" to your brain! It uses key words, symbols, pictures, and color to encourage a free flow of ideas and help the brain make new connections.[2]

FYI...

Walt Disney originally conceived the idea of storyboarding as a way to keep track of the thousands of drawings necessary for his animated films.[2]

A mind map, simply put, is a "hub and spoke" method of developing concepts. Draw a circle in the center of a piece of poster board. Write the goal of your training session in the circle. Draw lines extending from the circle and write your learning objectives on those lines. Continue to add "spokes" (or lines) from your learning objectives until all the information is covered. If you are more comfortable using technology, there is software that allows you to create mind maps on a computer.

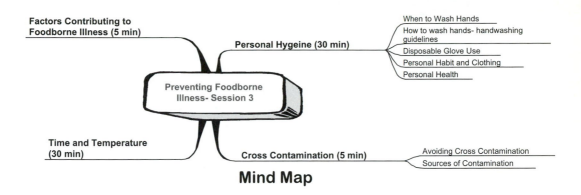

Mind Map

An Example... Developing the Content - Turnover training seminar

Note: All the examples in the chapter build on the same training need.

You are facing a problem with employee turnover, and you are looking for ways to reduce this problem. You have already:

- Created a needs analysis to show where problems are in the business
- Developed preliminary goals and objectives of what you want to accomplish.

You bring together the training manager, human resources director, and training developers to brainstorm a list of things you want to accomplish with the training.

From this group interaction you come up with the following ideas:

■ How training impacts employee satisfaction	■ Knowing what tools are available for hiring and training
■ Aces in places	■ Behavioral interviewing
■ Hiring the right employee	■ Building a team
■ Recruitment strategies	■ Orientation
■ Specific questions to ask in an interview	■ Consistent training for every employee
■ Ways to recognize employees	■ Company recognition programs.

ORGANIZING YOUR INFORMATION

Once you have all your data, begin to organize the information by grouping similar items together. Any key points that have too much information should be broken down into separate points. The goal in this step is to organize all the information you have collected during your research and brainstorming exercises. Ensure that the points flow smoothly from one to the next.

Prioritize the data in order of importance. You may want to have another trainer or subject matter expert assist you to obtain their unique perspectives on the material. Many trainers choose to prioritize information based on how it relates back to the business. For example, if your company is a provider of a service, customer or guest issues should be higher on the list of priorities than issues dealing with administrative processes.

An Example... Developing the Content - Turnover training seminar

You have brainstormed different topics to address employee turnover. Now it's time to organize and group the information together by topic.

Recruiting:

- Hiring the right employee
- Tools for recruiting
- Aces in places
- Recruitment strategies
- Behavioral interviewing process
- Asking the right questions.

Training:

- How training impacts employee satisfaction
- Orientation training
- Tools available for training
- Strategies for providing consistent training for everyone.

Recognition:

- Ways to recognize employees
- Company-wide recognition programs.

Review Training Goals and Objectives

Now that you have analyzed your options and chosen the most appropriate training method, you need to decide what you want the outcome of the training to be. As discussed in Chapter 2, you do this by creating training goals and writing your learning objectives. Consider this to be your encore presentation: your way of ensuring all your hard work will pay off and carry over into the workplace.

Goal Setting

Start by going back to your needs analysis. Why did you decide you needed the training in the first place? Take the time to develop clear, concise goal statements that answer the question "What do I want to achieve?" Refer to your goal statements periodically throughout your script writing to ensure you remain true to them.

Learning Objectives

Knowing "what" you want to achieve is only the first step. By writing your learning objectives you are showing how you are going to reach your goals. Objectives must be specific, clear, and measurable in order to be effective. Making objectives measurable is the biggest challenge. It is much easier to measure what trainees have learned after a performance when you specify up front what they have to be able to do in the training objectives.

Writing Measurable Objectives

Unclear Objective: The participant will understand how to set the table properly.

Measurable Objective: The learner will be able to set a banquet table with 100% accuracy.

The following table offers some suggestions taken from Bloom, B.S. (Ed.) (1956) Taxonomy of Educational Objectives. Use this chart when creating your objective statements.

Measurable Language

When Measuring...	Use statements beginning with:
Knowledge	define, describe, identify, name, outline, recognize, reproduce, or state.
Comprehension	convert, defend, estimate, explain, generalize, interpret, paraphrase, predict, summarize, or translate.
Application	apply, compute, construct, demonstrate, manipulate, modify, prepare, produce, or solve.
Analysis	analyze, break down, compare, contrast, diagram, differentiate, discriminate, distinguish, identify, illustrate, or separate.
Synthesis	categorize, combine, devise, design, generate, plan, rearrange, reorganize, revise, rewrite, or summarize.
Evaluation (Judgment)	appraise, compare, conclude, contrast, create, criticize, evaluate, explain, interpret, or justify.

Some terms do not appear in this list including: understand, comprehend, and think. These terms are not measurable and should not be used when writing measurable objectives.

CREATING AN OUTLINE

Now that you have grouped the information into broad topics, you need to prioritize them and place them into a working outline. List the major categories first and list key concepts under each category as subcategories. Use your learning objectives as a check and balance to ensure everything has been covered.

An Example... Developing the Content - Turnover training seminar

Place items in an outline, key concepts first. Identify specific points under each key concept.

I. Recruiting

A. Hiring the right employee:

1. Job descriptions

2. Special requirements

3. Team needs

B. Aces in places (matching the right person/skills to the right job)

C. Tools for recruiting:

1. Company application process

2. Behavioral interview process

3. Behavioral questions

4. Personality profile test

D. Recruitment strategies:

1. Places to recruit

2. When to recruit

3. Use of recruitment cards

II. Training

A. How training impacts employee satisfaction:

1. Training builds confidence

2. Training improves performance

3. Training develops employees

B. Orientation Training:

1. Critical to conduct on first day

2. Sets the tone for the rest of employee's tenure with the company

3. Introduces employee to company and policies

(continued)

An Example... Developing the Content (continued)

C. Tools available for training:(continued)

   1. Training programs

   2. Training resources

   3. Technology

D. Strategies for providing consistent training for everyone:

   1. Training plan for every employee

   2. Certified employee trainer program

   3. Short, ongoing training sessions

III. Recognition

A. Ways to recognize employees:

   1. Suggestions for informal recognition

B. Company-wide recognition programs:

   1. Company incentive programs

   2. Monthly, quarterly, and annual formal recognition programs

In an attempt to get a large volume of training developed and presented, trainers often rush the process. This results in trying to cram too much information into too little time, and not taking the time to identify the audience. It is important to get input from both potential audience members and their supervisors.

Use Subject Matter Experts

While you are developing the content of your script you may find you are unclear about one of your topics. If researching the topic does not answer your questions, you may want to ask an expert on the subject. You will most likely have only one opportunity to get information from a **subject matter expert (SME).** Be prepared by writing down specific questions you want to ask or having a list of items you want more information about. Make the most of any opportunity you may have to speak with a subject matter expert.

TRAINER TERMS

Subject Matter Expert (SME) – someone who has expert knowledge about a given topic or given skill

Another approach when seeking out a subject matter expert is to complete your training script and then ask him or her to read it for verification. Be specific in telling him or her what you would like attention paid to. This helps provide you with feedback that is useful and relevant. One possible downfall to this approach is you may have to do major rewriting on your materials.

Guidelines for Working with a Subject Matter Expert

1. Review topics you will want to expand and what information you will need from subject matter experts BEFORE you contact them. This helps ensure you are asking the right people for the information you need.

2. Identify subject matter experts based on the information you need.

3. Contact your subject matter experts and explain exactly what the project is and what it is you are asking them to do. Be specific.

4. Once they have agreed to help with the topic, the next step is to set up a time when you would be able to meet or talk.

5. Prepare for the meeting. Prepare a list of questions for them to answer. If you are having them review work to identify the mission or incorrect information, send it to them before the meeting so they can prepare.

6. Conduct the meeting. Be prepared. You don't want to waste the subject matter expert's time.

7. Once the meeting is complete, ask the person if you can contact him or her if there are future questions. In many cases, it will require more than one meeting to get all the information.

8.   Sort through the information you have gathered. Incorporate it into your training information. You may not use all the information, but if the subject matter expert feels a certain piece of information is critical, you need to consider it even if you don't agree.

9.   As a follow-up and a thank you, you may want to send the subject matter expert a copy of the finished script.

Trainers sometimes think the subject matter expert knows the content so they know how to write the training. This is not always the case. You must know what questions to ask regarding the content. When they respond and give their key points, take notes and make sure you include them in your training.

MAKING THE TRAINING SCHEDULE

The next step is to make a schedule for training. Now that you know the basic content you need to cover, how much time do you have to present the information? The training methods you use and the structure of activities, exercises, and breaks will depend on the time you have available. Creating a schedule will help keep you on track. Start this process by answering the following questions:

■ How much time do I have available to train?

■ How much time do I need on each section?

■ How long should I allow for breaks and lunch?

■ What games and activities are being included and how long will they take?

Based on your estimates, go through your outline and assign a time limit to each section. Finding time for training and understanding when people learn the best are an important part of creating your training schedule.

An Example... Developing the Content - Turnover training seminar

Assign time estimates to items in your outline.

I. Recruiting — 4 hours 10 minutes

A. Hiring the right employee: **1 hour**

    1. Job descriptions - **25 minutes**

    2. Special requirements - **10 minutes**

    3. Team needs - **25 minutes**

B. Aces in places (matching the right person to the right job) **10 minutes**

C. Tools for recruiting: **2 hours**

    1. Company application process - **15 minutes**

    2. Behavioral interview process - **1 hour**

    3. Behavioral questions - **30 minutes**

    4. Personality profile test - **15 minutes**

D. Recruitment strategies: **1 hour**

    1. Places to recruit - **30 minutes**

    2. When to recruit - **15 minutes**

    3. Use of recruitment cards - **15 minutes**

II. Training — 2 hours 15 minutes

A. How training impacts employee satisfaction: **30 minutes**

    1. Training builds confidence - **10 minutes**

    2. Training improves performance - **10 minutes**

    3. Training develops employees - **10 minutes**

(continued)

B. Orientation Training: **1 hour 45 minutes**   **(continued)**

    1. Critical to conduct on first day - **30 minutes**

    2. Sets the tone for the rest of employee's tenure with the company -**45 minutes**

    3. Introduces employee to company and policies - **30 minutes**

Energy Levels

When writing a training schedule, you need to keep in mind how energy levels vary throughout the day.

First Thing in the Morning

Audience members are still focused on things from home or they may still be sleepy. It's important to conduct activities that focus everyone on the day's events and get them energized.

Just before Lunch

Everyone is getting hungry and that causes energy levels to decrease. Use more physical activities around this time of day to keep everyone's mind on the topic.

After Lunch

One of the most difficult times of day to deliver a training performance is right after lunch. To help keep your audience alert during this time, you are going to need a high level of energy! Things you may want to try include:

- Facilitating a group activity
- Playing music
- Having frequent breaks throughout the afternoon.

Toward the End of the Day

People begin to feel overwhelmed with information and their minds are getting tired. Don't present key concepts or critical content late in the day. The audience will not be able to fully grasp them.

FYI...

Today's learner learns best in short sittings, 1-2 hours, with activities.

Great actors realize one of the most important things they can do is pace themselves and organize the training to minimize dips in energy.

Finding Time for Training

One of the greatest challenges of training in any work environment is finding time for training. While intellectually everyone agrees training is important, necessary, and an investment, we are constantly challenged to find ways to fit it into an already busy schedule. Strategies to get the training done (when time is at a premium) include continual training sessions, weekend seminars, brown bag forums, and utilizing pre- and post-work effectively.

Continual "short" training sessions

Create several short consecutive training sessions rather than a single, one- or two-day training session. This is beneficial for both the learner and the company. It allows training to occur without reducing productivity.

An Example...

You want to conduct supervisory skills training for some of the line-level employees in the service department. Rather than give them all the information at once, you would like to give them a topic, provide some directions, then let them practice the new skill before moving on to the next topic. You set up a class for two hours every Tuesday morning. In each session, you present a different topic within your supervisory skills training program. At the end of each session, you provide the audience with directions on incorporating or practicing the lesson as they return to their jobs for the next week. At the beginning of the next session, review the experiences the audience had involving last week's topic. Present the next topic and repeat the process all over again.

Weekend Seminars

A new trend in training is weekend seminars. This is especially effective when you can tie in personal growth topics as well. If you are going to utilize this type setting, always consider "WIIFM" or "What's In It For Me?" If the employee is

TRAINER TERMS

Soft Skills Training –
term that refers to training on topics such as communication, problem solving, leadership, and other skills. They are typically viewed as less tangible or concrete.

giving up a weekend, what is the perceived value? If the audience is putting in their own time, how will the training benefit them personally?

An Example...

There are many major changes taking place in your organization. The executives in their annual meeting rewrote the corporate mission and agreed to some initiatives that take the company in a new direction. Their plan is going to create some job redesign, introduce some new practices, and include a new quality program. The managers in the company need to get a handle on all the new things and how to manage all the changes. During a weekend training retreat, you blend change management training with experiential learning activities to provide the managers with the information they need to know and skills/tools to effectively implement the changes in their departments.

Brown Bag Forum/Learn with Lunch Programs

Leadership training, **soft skills training**, personal topics, and awareness training lend themselves very well to short time frames in a more informal environment. When training time is scarce, consider one of these luncheon training meetings. You will need to notify your audience if lunch is provided or if they need to bring a sack lunch. At a minimum, you will want to provide beverages.

An Example...

You are planning a short training session on personal safety. You design the training to be more of a dialogue where the trainees have the opportunity to share experiences. This is a perfect type training to do in a more casual setting or over lunch. You will want to provide, ahead of time if possible, a handout/outline for the discussion.

Pre-/Post-Work

Another way to cut down on actual class time is to either have trainees do "pre-work" before coming to the training session or "post-work" after training is complete. **Pre-work** allows the trainee to "ramp-up" quicker by gaining information on the subject before coming to class. **Post-work** allows the trainee to reinforce what was learned and utilize it when they are back on the job. Examples of pre-/post-work can include having trainees:

- Read books, manuals, or best practices guides
- Complete questionnaires
- Complete assignments in a workbook you have designed
- Seek out information from their supervisors based on questions they have received from you.

These are just some examples. The types of pre-/post-work activities that can be assigned are endless.

An Example...

Pre-work: You are conducting a training session on time management. Have the audience keep a journal for one week, recording their activities as they go through their days. Require them to bring this journal to class. Use this journal as the basis for helping them identify areas of opportunity, priorities, and how to organize their time. As the training class is presented, they could refer back to their list, identifying trouble spots!

Post-work: You conducted a training class on goal setting. By the end of the class, everyone was required to set three goals. The post-work is to accomplish the goals over the next three months. As part of the post-work, you required them to meet with their supervisor to discuss progress monthly.

TYPES OF TRAINING

Before you jump into writing your script, you must first understand the different types of training and training methods available to you. The skills you are trying to teach and the type of audience you are teaching dictate the method you will use. Many of these types are traditional and familiar. Others use newer methods and unique techniques.

One-on-One Training

One-on-one training is a more traditional type of training in which a trainer spends individual time with the trainee. This can sometimes be referred to as "OJT" or On the Job Training.

In this type of training:

- Specific **hard skills** are taught

- The training may occur over a period of time

- There will be practice time in between training sessions.

One-on-one training will create both benefits and challenges. The benefit is having the opportunity to teach an individual using the specific style that best suits him or her. This helps the trainee to learn more quickly. The rules around creativity, learning styles, and how to make training sticky still apply.

The challenge you face in one-on-one training is the loss of the richness of group dynamics. In other words, the learner only has what you tell them to learn from. In a group setting the experiences of the various participants are shared and trainees learn from one another. It is also more challenging to keep your energy level up and to keep the training interesting. The more you can incorporate creativity into the training and customize it to suit the needs of the learner, the more successful you will be.

Peer Mentoring

Peer mentoring involves putting an experienced person, a mentor, with a new employee. Often the learning that takes place in this type of training is more informal. The training often occurs during conversations between the mentor and the employee, the trainee and a co-worker, or through some type of storytelling by the mentor. Peer mentoring can be planned or happen naturally.

An Example...

The chef in the kitchen has a new trainee he wants to teach how to make the signature or specialty sauce of the restaurant. Using a standardized recipe, the chef shows his trainee, step by step, the procedure for preparing the sauce. Once he has shown this to his trainee, the trainee demonstrates what he has learned from the chef. The chef is able to critique the trainee's procedures and technique immediately and make suggestions for improvement next time!

Self-Directed or Individual Development Training

Many studies have proven much of the training in the workplace is self- directed. Trainees learn at their own pace through discovery, reading, asking questions, and practicing. This method is very effective when you want your trainees to seek out information on their own. It's also effective when you want your trainees to practice **discovery learning**.

TRAINER TERMS

Discovery Learning –
describes learning done by having the learner seek out answers and information from books, observations, or other methods through a series of questions or activities

Individual development training programs involve:

- Trainers facilitating or helping in the learning process

- Trainers recording progress, checking in at key points, and ensuring the trainee is progressing

- Trainees using a specific program or outline designed for their learning needs. The program provides them with direction on how the learning process should be experienced.

If you choose to use this method of training, be sure to:

- Clarify your expectations with the trainee

- Provide clear instructions on how to complete the program

- Determine how you will know when the trainee has completed the program

- Have tools for measuring the trainee's knowledge on the contents of the program.

Individual development training programs are beneficial because they allow the trainee to choose when they will do their learning. The challenge of this type training is the lack of a structured environment. This can make it difficult for some trainees to complete their training tasks.

An Example...

Angela, an hourly supervisor in Customer Service, has expressed an interest in moving up in the organization. She indicated she would like to move into a salaried management position within her department. The first step of her training involves a workbook broken into several sections. Each section of the workbook includes information and skills required for a Customer Service

(continued)

Manager. There are questions, exercises, and activities Angela will need to complete throughout the workbook. Angela will have a time frame in which she must complete the program. As the trainer, you must schedule regular meetings with her to check progress and answer any questions she may have.

Training Moments

Sometimes referred to as teaching moments or moments of truth, training moments are a type of informal training. A training moment is simply an interaction between you and an employee, where you have observed a behavior and are communicating how it can be improved upon. You can also use training moments to reinforce positive behavior. Training moments are usually unplanned and can occur at any time, in any place. They also provide a great way to focus on continuous improvement.

An Example...

You are a trainer in a hotel. You happen to be walking through the lobby when you notice an interaction between a guest and Julie, one of the employees that just attended your Customer Service training class. You pause to listen. While observing, you notice Julie does a great job interacting with the guest but is not using the guest's name, one of the things hotel management feels is very important. You wait until the interaction is over and the guest has left. You approach Julie and tell her what a great job she did with the guest. Then you ask her (based on what she learned in the Customer Service class) what she might improve on. Immediately she smiles and says she forgot to use the guest's name! You congratulate Julie for thinking so quickly and remind her again of how important it is to use the guest's name.

Training Through Technology

This emerging method of training redefines the role of training. Technology has reinvented the way a company can deliver ideas, information, and best practices. It is a method that takes a learner-centered approach by delivering

TRAINER TERMS

Just-in-time training –
quick response training delivered at the moment it is needed

training in a flexible and interactive way. The benefit of this type training is it provides **just-in-time training**. It allows learners to train when and how they want. The challenges we face with technological training include trainers understanding the technology, the costs, and the acceptance of change. Like most innovations, in the early stages, this method is struggling to define itself. One thing is certain, however: Technology is here to stay. Some more common emerging technology-based training activities include:

■ Computer-based simulations

■ E-book learning

■ Computerized exams and quizzes

■ Research and reference using the Internet.

These technology-based forms of training can be expensive to develop and take skilled people to implement the products. They can however be very cost effective if you need to train a large number of people on the same information, have people in many different locations who need training, or have materials that change infrequently. The technology is evolving to be more user friendly and easier to update by people with average computer skills.

Group Training

Group training is a method of training involving three or more people being trained simultaneously. Group training is extremely effective when you want to:

■ Roll out new company initiatives

■ Get group buy-in to a concept

■ Provide opportunities for different groups to work together or interact with one another

■ Encourage teamwork

■ Encourage competition (using simulation exercises).

The majority of this book is dedicated to this group training. Group training allows people to interact and communicate with each other. It can be an effective way to train a large group of people at one time and makes good use of trainer resources. However, if the group is too big, group training can be less personal. Some people may feel uncomfortable sharing their ideas or asking questions in a large group setting.

Overview of Types of Training				
Type of Training	**Involves**	**Advantages**	**Disadvantages**	**Example**
One-on-one	Trainers spending individual time with trainee	Training tailored to the learner	Loss of the richness of group dynamics	Teaching a line-level associate how to perform a specific task on the job.
Self-Directed/ Individual Development	Trainee learns at own pace through discovery	Trainee chooses when and how learning occurs	Lack of structured environment can be a challenge for some	Having trainee use questions to research and learn about company policies.
Training Moments	Informal coaching at the time of action	Great way to focus on continuous improvement	If environment isn't set up for this type coaching, some may get defensive	A supervisor observing a line-level associate incorrectly performing a task and re-teaching him or her on the spot.
Training Through Technology	Learn using a computer and specific courseware and programs	Delivers the training when the trainee needs it	It's still in the early stages of defining what it is and how it should be used	Having a trainee learn how to utilize a program by using an on-line tutorial.
Group Training	Three or more people trained simultaneously in a learning environment	Provides opportunities for different groups to work together	Group process loses some individualized attention for group members	Having managers attend a diversity training session where group interaction enhances the experience.

OFF THE SHELF TRAINING

Before you begin with your script development, you may want to consider using some form of **off the shelf** training. There may be occasions where you want to purchase or use training that has already been created. Using off the shelf training materials may help you

save training money in the long run by eliminating the time and effort involved in developing and creating materials. Consider using off the shelf training when it covers basic information your users must know. It may be cheaper to buy a program on basic customer service skills than develop your own. Be sure your training budget allows for this type training.

Off the shelf training can come from internal sources (your own company) or external sources (another company or person). When using these types programs, you will still want to customize the training to fit your training needs. When customizing off the shelf training, it's important to remember the following:

- Never alter the main points or message of the materials.
- Do not try to change the message for a purpose different from what was intended.
- Always give credit where credit is due. Don't use someone else's training materials/script and then try to pass it off as your own.

Several large companies create their own off the shelf training programs. These programs may have very specific guidelines for you to follow. They can be so specific as to require you to follow a pre-written script, timelines, and activities. This type of training may be mandated from your company.

An Example...

You need to do a training class on telephone etiquette. You don't have the time or expertise to create the content yourself so you decide to purchase an off the shelf program. You select a great program that includes videotape, a facilitator's guide and a participant's workbook. They have been provided to you on a computer compact disk (CD). The CD program allows you to

(continued)

An Example... (continued)

customize it for your company. Each key concept of the training is chunked into a separate section. The program includes the following:

- Fun with phones
- It's all about etiquette
- They really do hear you smile
- Do's and don'ts
- Practice, practice, practice
- Scripting for success.

You can choose which modules or sections you want to use and disregard the rest. You can also customize the activities to current issues taking place in your company.

Whichever methods you choose to use in your training, you should have the basic outline of materials to be covered and the basic schedule you will follow when doing the performance. You're ready to develop the content and decide how to present your information.

REFERENCES

1. Wycoff, Joyce. *Mind Mapping: Your Personal Guide to Exploring Creativity and Problem Solving.* Berkeley Books. June 1991.

2. Capodagli, Bill, and Jackson, Lynn. *The Disney Way.* McGraw-Hill, New York, 1999.

SKILL BUILDERS

1. Analyze the brainstorming methods given in this chapter. Describe the pros and cons for each.

2.   Develop a sample training schedule; be sure to include time for content and breaks.

3.   Discuss when it is appropriate to use more than one type of training.

4.   Make a list of decisions rules for scheduling training. After completing, list the key influence on choosing the optimal time choice.

5.   Find an "off the shelf" package on the Internet. Describe the training methods, training goals, and objectives. Make a list of questions you have about the product.

Chapter 6

DEVELOPING THE SCRIPT

PART 2: ELEMENTS OF THE PERFORMANCE

Learning which involves the whole person of the learner, feelings as well as intellect, is the most lasting and pervasive. — Carl Rogers

IN THIS CHAPTER:

- **Create Mini-Lessons**
- **Engaging the Audience**
- **A Guide to A/V Equipment**
- **Make Training Fun**
- **Creative Training Ideas**
- **Games and Activities**
- **Opening and Closing the Session**
- **When You Get Stuck During Scripting**
- **Reference**
- **Skill Builders**

The second part of script writing is to develop the performance. In Part 1, you determined the content, wrote goals and objectives to match the content, organized it into sections, assigned a timeframe to each part, and looked at the different methods of presenting the information. In Part 2, you begin to plan your performance in detail.

Part 2: Elements of the Performance – Chapter 6

Develop Mini-Lessons for Each Key Point Area	■ Use your outline as a template and begin to create small lesson chunks.
Decide How to Present the Information	■ Consider using visuals ■ Gather written materials ■ Use creative thinking methods and exercises ■ Schedule games and activities.
Engage the Learner	■ Use methods that make learning fun for the users ■ Use humor appropriately.
Include Measurement	■ Thread performance checks that measure learning throughout the training session ■ Use a variety of measurement tools.
Open and Close the Session	■ Plan session openings and closings ■ Incorporate icebreakers and set expectations ■ Close the session on a high note.

CREATE MINI-LESSONS

Use your detailed outline with timelines from Chapter 5 as your template. Begin by taking a section of your training and turning it into a short lesson. Decide how you are going to present your key points and what support materials you need to develop. This becomes your map of the performance. Be sure to keep the audience in mind when determining presentation formats. You want to keep them thinking and learning. Before you jump into writing your script, you need to answer these three questions:

- What can you add to the script to help the audience relate what they learn back to their jobs or lives?

- What can you add to the script to help the transfer of learning occur in the workplace? In other words, how does the learner apply what he or she were taught?

- What can you add to the script to make the training sticky? In other words, more than trying something new once or twice, how do they consistently apply the new learning over time?

An Example: Developing the Content – Turnover training seminar

Take a section of your outline and break it down into a mini-lesson, including key information to cover, length of time, how you will present it, and what materials you need to develop.

Recruiting: 4 hours 30 minutes

Hiring the right employee: 1 hour

Topic Area	Key Information	Length of Time	Presentation Method	Materials Needed
1. Job descriptions	■ Using existing job descriptions ■ How to find the right people	30 minutes	■ PowerPoint® ■ Sample job descriptions	■ Sample job descriptions ■ PowerPoint® printouts
2. Special needs	■ Coordinating with department heads	10 minutes	■ PowerPoint®	■ PowerPoint® printouts
3. Team needs	■ Company culture	10 minutes	■ PowerPoint®	■ PowerPoint® printouts
4. Aces in places (matching the right person to the right job)	■ Program mechanics	10 minutes	■ PowerPoint®	■ PowerPoint® printouts

(continued)

Tools for Recruiting: 3 hours 30 minutes

Topic Area	Key Information	Length of Time	Presentation Method	Materials Needed
1. Company application process	■ Information included on application ■ Key information to look for	15 minutes	■ Discussion using application form	■ Application form
2. Behavioral interview process	■ How to conduct an interview ■ Things to look for - verbal and nonverbal messages ■ Positive/ negative behaviors	1 ½ hours	■ Discussion ■ View 3 excerpts from videotaped interviews – audience to evaluate candidate based on checklist and job descriptions	■ Videotaped interviews ■ Review sheet ■ Handout on things to look for - verbal/ nonverbal ■ Outline of the interview process - checklist
3. Behavioral questions	■ Questions to ask ■ Responses to look for	1 ½ hours	■ Role play mock interviews – divide class into groups of 4, have 2 people act out role of interviewer/ candidate and 2 people observe	■ Handout on questions ■ Review sheet on interviewing ■ Role-play scenarios
4. Personality profile test	■ Profile curves ■ Different personality types ■ What we learn	15 minutes	■ PowerPoint® ■ Profile test summary sheet	■ PowerPoint® printouts ■ Profile summary sheet

ENGAGING THE AUDIENCE

When trainers first begin training, their goal is often to provide information in the quickest, most *efficient* way. While this is important, we have to look at being *efficient* AND *effective*. Training that engages the mind, body, and emotions of the audience can create sticky training.

Audience-Centered Techniques

Effective trainers understand audience-centered training techniques can have a positive, long-lasting impact on the participants. It is the total experience that achieves the best results. This experience taps into the memory, emotions, and creativity of the audience. It engages the five senses and requires active participation of each audience member.

Memory and Learning

Memory is created by input from our senses to our brain. If something is determined to be important by the conscious or subconscious mind, it's put into memory. It first goes to short-term memory and then to long-term memory. This determination is based on interest, relevance, and impact. A successful trainer understands this and strives to create a session that not only teaches information, but also presents it in a way that enhances the chances for the audience to retain it in their memory. This will allow the learner to recall it when he or she is back in the workplace.

Emotion and Learning

Recent studies in neuroscience show proof that there is a direct relationship between emotion and reason. It has been discovered that the part of the brain involved in processing emotions is the same part involved in processing memory. Based on this, the more the learner is emotionally engaged, the more likely he or she is to remember what is being taught. Training that encourages the audience to utilize all five senses helps tap emotion.

Involving the Senses Can Help Learners Keep Their Focus

You may find when you are training on a subject that involves several topics your audience may have difficulty shifting from topic to topic. One strategy to help them shift to a new topic is to do a physical activity. The activity can be done either just before the presentation of the new topic or during it. Using a physical activity can help the learner change his or her mental focus.

Create Personal Links to Key Concepts

A good way to bring emotion into the learning environment is to create personal links between the topic and your audience whenever possible. Ways you can do this include:

- Link the topic to a real-life situation or example.
    - Consider you are presenting a training performance on Sexual Harassment in the Workplace. You are discussing the importance of not using words that offend people and how using them can be a form of sexual harassment. You share a story you read in the newspaper about a woman who sued her boss for harassment. The boss consistently used offensive language even though the woman asked him on many occasions to stop. The more she asked, the worse he got. She finally went to see a lawyer and sued her boss for sexual harassment. She won $750,000.
- Explain how the topic relates to those in the audience.
    - Consider you are doing a chemical safety training performance. You are reviewing what can happen if chemical safety procedures are not followed. You explain how an employee, in an attempt to make his job easier, mixed two chemicals together. The chemicals immediately started reacting and gave off a vapor. The employee got very ill and had to be rushed to the hospital. Had his co-workers not reacted so quickly, the employee could have died because the vapor was deadly. Convey to your audience how important it is to follow proper chemical safety procedures or they too could find themselves in a dangerous situation.
- Ask the audience how they think this topic relates to them.
    - After you have just presented a training performance on the Top Ten Leadership Traits, ask your audience how these traits relate to them. Encourage discussion of how these traits are necessary in their current position or in a position they are trying to obtain.

Repetition Is Key

Repeating key concepts helps training remain in the learner's memory. The more times people hear it, see it, and feel it, the greater the chance of them remembering it! Use multiple forms of reviewing to maximize the chance of retention.

The Flow of the Performance

Timing can be everything during a performance. When designing your training, you need to present your information in small segments. There are several strategies for creating a good performance.

Change Topics and Tasks Frequently

A strategy to help keep your audience engaged is to change or break up your topic every 15-20 minutes. With people's attention spans getting shorter, it is critical to "fast feed" information to your audience. Chunk your information into small digestible pieces. During your performance, use **energizers** and learning activities to break up large topics or to transition to a different topic.

Energizers can be used:

- Any time the energy level of the audience is low
- Just before watching a video
- After lunch
- To break up long or complicated training topics.

TRAINER TERMS

Energizer –
short activity designed to increase the energy level of the audience

You can create your own energizers or purchase books that have hundreds of energizers. Appendix A contains a list of resources for energizers.

Sample Energizer

Table Group Storytelling: Hand one person at each table a ball. Have that person start a story. After one minute, ask him or her to toss the ball to the next person at the table who continues the story. Do this until everyone at the table has had a turn. It's a great way to lighten the mood and get everyone participating!

Don't Change Your Focus Abruptly

While you want to keep the flow of the performance changing, trying to discuss several topics at once can confuse your audience. Fully discuss all the aspects of one concept before moving onto the next. Allow them to ask questions about each topic prior to moving forward. Doing this will help your audience grasp the information more easily and ensure they fully understand the topic. When presenting long topics, you can keep the audience's focus by shifting the *way* you present the information.

Keep Focused on the Goal

In the script development process, it is important to stay organized and focused on your main points. Be specific. Keep within the scope of your goals and learning objectives. Including irrelevant information to the script can confuse the audience and negatively impact the training. By staying focused and organized, you will produce a solid training performance. If you want to provide additional information, put it in an appendix or a separate document.

Trainers often include more information than needed. When this happens, your audience can get lost in all the information and miss the key points you want them to take away from the session.

Keep it simple.

A Guide to A/V Equipment

When you design your script, you need to consider what types of audio/visual (A/V) equipment you may want to use to get your message across. A/Vs may range from a simple whiteboard to a laser and lights show. It is important that your A/V choices be appropriate for your training performance. Your A/Vs may be the difference between wide-awake learners and someone snoozing in the back row. For purposes of discussion, let's look at the most common high-tech and low-tech A/V choices.

Low-tech A/V Equipment

Low-tech A/V equipment includes whiteboards and chalkboards, flip charts, and overhead projectors and transparencies. These are traditional training tools that still have a place in our technology-filled world.

Whiteboards and chalkboards

Whiteboards and chalkboards are a traditional tool most of us are familiar with from childhood. Drawing a picture and writing key information on the board can be a very effective way to help people grasp a concept. Whiteboards and chalkboards are relatively inexpensive to install. Whiteboards require special markers and are less messy than chalkboards.

Flip Charts

Flip charts are still one of the most versatile training tools actors have at their disposal. They are great for capturing answers to questions, brainstorming in groups, and displaying key concepts. Simply a large pad of paper on a stand, flip charts are easy to transport and set up, you can refer back to information that has been written, and you don't run out of space as you would with a whiteboard or chalkboard.

Transparencies/Overhead Projectors

Transparencies are typically created on a computer and then printed on clear, plastic overhead sheets. These sheets are then placed on an overhead projector and displayed on a white screen or even a wall. They are great for showing spreadsheets, columns of numbers, and technical information. They are relatively easy to prepare and project a professional image.
Transparencies are also used as a backup option when more high-tech A/V fails.

Don't put too much information on a transparency. Be sure the words or graphics are large enough for everyone in the room to see!

Low-tech in a High-tech Society

Many actors question why they should use low-tech A/V aids in a high-tech society. Don't be afraid or embarrassed to use the low-tech A/V aids. There are many reasons why:

■ If something goes wrong with a projector or a computer, flip charts or overheads are a great backup.

■ If all you use is PowerPoint® slides, your audience will soon get bored and the slides will lose their impact. The key to success is using a variety of methods to get your message across.

There are also things high-tech A/V can't accomplish; but low-tech A/V can including:

■ **Gallery walk –** If you have recorded many ideas on flip charts, you can place them around the room and have the audience view them. This is especially useful when voting on ideas and concepts.

■ **Review –** Similar to the gallery walk, placing flip charts around the room is a great way for the audience to review key concepts.

■ **Reminders throughout training class –** The main concepts you presented at the

> FYI...
>
> When considering low-tech visual aids, ask the questions:
>
> ■ Are they professional?
>
> ■ Are they user friendly and easy to read?
>
> ■ Are they relevant to the discussion?

beginning of class may need to be referred back to frequently. Flip charts are a great way to do that by placing them around the room.

When trainers are using flip charts, they tend to face and talk to the flip chart rather than the audience. Look at your flip chart, point to it, and then turn and talk to your audience!

High-tech A/V Equipment

TV/VCRs, CD players, electronic whiteboads, LCD projectors, and/or rear screen projectors have become pivotal pieces of equipment for many performers. Don't forget to secure your tech support when planning for your training session. This is the part of your planning where assembly and batteries are required, or at least a long extension cord.

Electronic Flip Charts and Whiteboards

People are always looking for ways to make a good thing better, and this includes whiteboards and flip charts. There are special flip chart boards, markers, and recording devices available that allow you to print your flip charts, project the images you draw on the flip chart onto a large screen, and download information into your computer. An **electronic whiteboard** is the standard term for a special board you use to save dry erase marker notes to a connected computer. An **interactive whiteboard** is the term for a product on which you display your computer desktop and then interact at the board with the information – you can open applications, navigate websites, and write and save whiteboard notes. On some whiteboards with plasma displays, you can connect your computer to the board and it displays the computer screen. Any contact with the screen acts like the mouse on your computer.

Video with TV/VCR

Videos are a great way to illustrate a subject. If done well, videos are interesting, entertaining, and easy to use. The acceptable length for a video is typically 15-20 minutes. Longer videos should be chunked into short clips with discussion and activity in between each clip. Doing this will help you keep your audience's attention. When using videos, enhance their impact by doing the following:

- Preview the tape before showing it to the audience. It is important to know that the condition of the tape is good and that the tape contains what you want to show.

- Set up the video before showing it to your audience by discussing its overall message. Explain to the audience what points to watch for.

- After viewing the video, discuss the important points. To encourage retention, ask questions about what they learned.

CD Player and Music

CD players are used to play music in the learning environment. They can be internal and tied into an existing built-in speaker system or stand-alone units. Music can be used as background for certain activities, to entertain and motivate during breaks, and to set the tone for a performance. Music can be used to change the mood of your audience. It can add energy, it can calm a group down, or it can be used to bring back memories. Ultimately, it is used to touch the emotions of the audience.

> **FYI...**
> Never leave the stage when a video is playing. Things can go wrong with the technology and you need to be there to take care of it. Also, watching the video with your audience helps refresh the key points in your mind.

Use music:

- When opening and closing your sessions
- During breaks and lunch
- When your audience is working on a project, reading an assignment, or working in a group
- To energize the group
- During games and simulations
- To get audience members into a certain frame of mind.

Projectors

LCD projectors are used to display whatever is on your computer screen onto a wall or screen. Some training facilities and rooms designed for larger presentations are equipped with **rear screen projection systems**. These operate on a similar basis to LCD in that they connect to a computer or VCR and project the image onto a large screen. The difference is the image is projected from behind the screen and is out of the audience's view.

One of the most commonly used tools with this is the Microsoft® PowerPoint® presentation. This type of presentation uses Microsoft® PowerPoint® software to create a slide show of important concepts. PowerPoint® presentations convey a professional image and are easy to use. You can learn more about using PowerPoint® in Chapter 7.

Whichever visual aids you choose, don't let the method overwhelm the point you are trying to make. Variety is important when using visual aids. Here are a few guidelines to consider when creating and using high-tech A/V aids:

- Use animation as a change of pace, not a steady diet
- Don't use so many **bells & whistles** that your message gets lost
- Make them user friendly and easy to understand
- Ensure they are relevant to the discussion.

T R A I N E R   T E R M S

Bells & Whistles –
   used to refer to adding graphics, pictures, sound, color, or backgrounds. Basically adding anything to enhance the presentation.

Summary Chart of Visual Aids

Type	Use	Advantages	Disadvantages
Whiteboard/ Chalkboard	Emphasize material Illustrate a point	Low cost, easy to use, and maintain	Cannot refer back to information that has been erased
Flip Charts	Capture answers during brainstorming Show key concepts to your audience	Easy to use, readily accessible, and versatile	May be difficult to see in large groups
Transparencies w/Overhead Projector	Show technical information	Easy to prepare and use	Not as versatile as others
Electronic Flip Charts and Whiteboards	Show videotapes during event	Good for capturing notes and ideas from the audience; eliminates people having to copy information from the board	Can be expensive; requires a computer
Interactive Whiteboards	The whiteboard acts as a touch-sensitive computer display	Good for demonstrating computer programs; excellent for use in distance-learning settings	Expensive investment in equipment
Video w/TV & VCR	Show videotapes during event	Great for illustrating subject	Lose audience's attention if too long
CD/CD Player	Play music during event	Reliable; great way to motivate audience	Can be distracting if used inappropriately
LCD Projectors	Utilize computer to illustrate key points of topic	Easy, professional, interesting	Disengages audience if this is only method utilized
Rear Screen Projectors	Same as LCD projector, only image projected from behind the screen	Audience doesn't see equipment; doesn't block view	More complicated to use

MAKE TRAINING FUN

Learning that is fun is learning that sticks. There are many things you can do to make the learning environment fun. But a word of caution: Know your audience. What you may think is fun may not be for them. Also be sure that in an attempt to have fun you do not offend any of your audience. Finally, you must manage the environment. If one of the audience members takes having fun to an extreme, you could lose the attention of your entire audience.

Use Brainteasers and Mental Stretching Exercises

Brainteasers and mental stretching exercises are great ways to get people going when the energy of the group is waning. They don't have to be related to the topic. One way to use them is as part of a break. Set up a competition among groups within the audience. Give the groups a brainteaser and a timeframe within which they must complete it. The group that gets all the items on the brainteaser correct the quickest wins a prize (usually candy or small inexpensive items)!

Have Candy on Hand

Have various candies on hand for recognitions or to use as prizes for various games and competitions. Some examples include:

- Lifesavers® – for the participant who finally answered when no one else would and "saved the day"!

- Snickers® – for the participant who effectively used humor and made everyone laugh!

- PayDay® – for the group who won a competition!

FYI...

Have individually wrapped hard candy or miniature candy bars on hand. If your audience seems to be losing energy, passing out candy may help as a "quick picker-upper"!

Use Props

Either you or your audience can use props. Props are a great way to help illustrate your message. For example, if you are teaching a class in fire safety and you are explaining how to use a fire extinguisher, have the fire extinguisher there to help the audience visualize the parts as you talk about them.

Props don't always have to be specifically related to a topic. If you were having a discussion on company procedures for coaching and counseling employees, you could put on a baseball hat that says coach and hang a whistle around your neck! To help you effectively use props, follow these guidelines:

- Use props sparingly. Too many or too frequent use could be construed by the audience as "hokey."

- Use props that would not be offensive to any person or groups of persons. If in doubt, don't use it!

- Rehearse with your props. Timing is everything! If the prop malfunctions or is used at the wrong time, it becomes ineffective!

- Keep props simple. They are not meant to cause you or your audience stress trying to figure them out!

The right props can help make training fun.

Bring Toys

Having toys around the room for audience members to play with can actually help people concentrate. Toys also enhance creativity. Multi-tasking is a large part of today's fast-paced lifestyle. Many of today's workers seem to be in perpetual motion. It is very difficult for them to slow down long enough to sit in a class. Toys can actually act as stress relievers for these audience members and give them something to do with their hands while listening. The key is to have the right type of toys. They should not be toys that make a lot of noise. They should not require so much concentration they take the learner's focus off the training session.

FYI...

To help manage the learning environment when using toys, set up the following rules with your audience ahead of time. When presenting these rules, keep it light and do it in a humorous way. You may say:

- "The toys came with me and they leave with me!"
- "The toys do not take flight in the room!"
- "Share with your neighbor!"

Some great toys to include in your session might be:

- Silly Putty®
- Swoosh balls
- Stress balls
- Lego® blocks
- Miniature stuffed animals
- Play Dough®
- Crayons and coloring books
- Colored paper and markers
- Balloons.

Use Animated Videos

Put an animated or cartoon video in the VCR and let it run prior to the start of class in the morning, during breaks, and at lunchtime. It's a great way to lighten up the minds of your learners for a few minutes!

Use Humor in Your Training

Using humor lowers the tension in the learning environment. It's also a great way to tap into the emotions of the learner. It also encourages creative thinking. Many trainers are afraid to use humor. They believe they don't know how to tell jokes or their jokes won't be funny to the audience. Humor doesn't necessarily have to mean telling jokes. It can be done through surprises and stories.

Humor Helps Create a Playful Atmosphere

The bottom line is to have a playful relationship with your audience. The best trainers encourage the whole group to get involved! Some ways to effectively use group humor include:

■ Creating group connections or "customs"

■ Recognizing the audience's attempts at humor

■ Having a strategy for those who take it too far.

An Example:

"I was facilitating a one-week management training class for a group with diverse ages, backgrounds, and experiences. One of my favorite toys in the classroom was a stuffed frog, and I jokingly told the class it was my toy. Later in the day the frog was gone, and I received a ransom note in its place! Throughout the week, I received pictures of the frog in various settings, letters from the frog, and the frog changed hands, attended after-class outings, and became a class mascot. The frog became a great bonding tool for the group, and we all had a great time with it!"

Carrying it Too Far— Sometimes people take a "joke" too far. You want everyone to enjoy themselves, but not at the expense of others. If members of the audience start "enjoying themselves too much" by using sarcasm, off-color humor, or politically incorrect humor, it's time to reel them back! Take control by:

■ Using a different tone of voice

■ Using more powerful body language

■ Using stern facial expressions.

You don't want to lose the positive impact of humor, but you need to take control of the environment. Those being disruptive know they are. If you allow them to get away with it they will continue. When they see that you are taking control, they will usually back off right away!

Use Interactive Storytelling

Telling a story and sharing personal experiences is another great way to help your audience learn and retain key concepts.

- Stories provide an imaginative reference point
- Stories tap into our emotions
- Stories provide a way to communicate messages people can relate to in a way that is relevant to them
- Stories help put people at ease
- Stories help get the audience's attention.

When we were children, stories helped us make sense of the world. As adults, stories are still a great way to help us make sense of an issue or topic. To make our storytelling successful, however, there are some rules you should follow:

- Stories need to be relevant to the topic. A story only has an impact if the audience can tie the story to the learning.
- The connection to the audience is stronger if your stories are based on your own personal experiences. This way you are telling *your* story as opposed to sharing another's story secondhand.

Have the learners create a story on the topic you are discussing. Give audience members colored paper, coloring books, crayons, markers, or other items you may want them to have. Have them draw a picture representing their view of a particular topic. This could also be done with small groups, drawing a group picture representing their view. Once they have completed their drawing, have them tell their story using their picture. This is a great way to get your audience sharing stories with one another.

CREATIVE TRAINING IDEAS

Creativity should be a scheduled part of every element in the training performance. One great way to help your performance connect with the audience is to add creative exercises. The more we can use creativity, the more creative we become. The more we can thread creativity throughout the training, the more creative our audience will be and the more willing they will be to learn new things. Specific exercises and techniques include:

- **Creative thinking exercises**—These exercises help participants see the limitations of past problem-solving approaches and can get the audience looking at things differently. They include physical exercises, paradigm problems, mind teasers, and puzzles. There are hundreds of books, websites, and classes to help you find or develop these exercises for your training.

- **Asking questions**—As children, we asked many questions as we tried to figure out the world. As we get older, we tend to be afraid to ask questions. You may need to teach the audience to ask questions again. When encouraging audience members to ask questions, guide them by teaching how to ask open-ended questions that start with words like why, how, what if, when, and who.

In business, asking questions has led to many innovations. In training, they might help the audience member understand and make connections.

Often facilitators tell their audience members to ask questions, and then shut them down when an audience member tries. It's important to remove the "fear" of asking questions by taking each one seriously and treating each person asking the questions with respect and genuine interest.

Creative Thinking Techniques

In addition to the creativity exercises, there are some creative thinking techniques that can be used throughout your script. These are especially good when you are teaching concepts that require changes from an audience member. Some creative thinking short-shorts might include the following.

Wild Ideas Exercise

Have audience members brainstorm solutions to a problem. Encourage them to come up with solutions that are "outside the box," or different from what would be safe and normal. Tell them to think in terms of solutions that are wild, ridiculous, and absurd. This helps to break down restrictive thinking.

Role Reversal

Have audience members come up with a problem or opportunity at work. Have them play the role of their supervisor or colleague. Ask them to act out how they think that supervisor or colleague would handle the situation. Encourage the audience to try to look at the situation from the perspective of the role they are playing.

"What If" Questions

Have audience members come up with a problem or opportunity. Have them ask "What if" questions around the issue. Using "What if...?" will help the audience members see different ways of looking at things.

Quiet Time

Once you ask a question about a certain problem or opportunity, your brain starts working on it. If you are constantly busy, your brain will not interrupt to provide you with a solution. Teach your audience members to set aside a few minutes every day to relax their mind and allow creative thoughts to develop. Ask your audience: "When do some of your best ideas come to you?"

- In the shower?
- When you're driving?
- When you're swimming in a pool?

Often, your best ideas come when you are doing routine tasks or when you are relaxing. These are examples of times when your brain was able to provide you with ideas or answers to questions. People often refer to these as an "idea out of the blue," but the reality is often your brain has been working on the issue for some time and it's the first opportunity it's had to be able to present it to you!

GAMES AND ACTIVITIES

Another important part of writing your script is to consider what types of games or activities you want in the performance. Games and activities are a great way to have fun—with a purpose. They can be great learning tools! Games can also provide action, experiential learning or real-life simulation. Make sure, however, that the activity fits your audience and topic. Use games and activities to:

- Help illustrate a key idea
- Provide your audience with practice
- Break up or energize a heavy topic.

Games

Games are most effective when they are challenging for the audience. They should not be so difficult that the audience can't succeed, nor so easy that everyone is bored.

Types of Games

Some types of games include:

TRAINER TERMS

Game –
a structured activity with a specific learning objective at the end

- **Action games**—These typically resemble real-life scenarios. May be group led or facilitator led.
- **Board games**—These use a board, dice, and cards and are patterned after board games you may have grown up with.
- **Card games**—May have quotes, facts, or definitions printed on the cards. They may be used like flash cards or may be patterned after traditional card games.

- **Experiential learning games—**
  Involves some type of physical activity or a "hands-on" approach for the audience.

- **Computer games—**Often resemble TV game shows or electronic versions of board games.

- **Computer simulation games—**
  Create real-life situations where participants have opportunities to make decisions and see results.

> **FYI...**
> **Keep in mind that audience members from other countries may not understand some of the rules of American games.**

Many companies have developed these types games for a wide variety of subjects. There is a reference list of some of these companies in Appendix A.

A major problem with having the audience play games: once the game is over the trainer may not provide the link back to the topic or the purpose of the game. The audience has a good time and then asks "So what? Why did we do it?" It's important to debrief the game and talk about the outcome as it relates to what you are discussing in the training performance.

When considering whether or not to use a game, ask yourself the following questions:

- What's the purpose of the game?
- Why use it?
- When will you use it or how will you incorporate it into your presentation?
- How many people can play it either individually, in small groups, or in a large group?
- How long will the game take?
- Do you understand how to use it?
- How much will it cost?

■ What technology, if any, is needed?

■ Do you have the physical space to do it?

When using a game, it is important to debrief the audience after it is over. Discuss with the audience what they learned from the game. Ask them questions about their experience and tie it back to the training. Ask the audience how they can apply what they have learned through the game in the workplace.

Activities

In addition to games, there are several other activities that can be used to enhance learning. Just like games, activities need to be tied to one or more of the key concepts of the training performance. Additionally, they must be appropriate for the audience.

Scenario-Based Training

This is a type of training where you write or create a situation and then have participants work through the situation. This type training is typically not done in the classroom. It takes place in settings as close to reality as possible. The more "props" you can provide, the better the activity.

Scenario-based training is common in military settings, police training, and fire safety. It can be very helpful in watching how a person performs in a given situation. Scenario-based training requires a tremendous amount of time and attention to detail in order to be successful.

Role Plays

Role plays are a great way to determine visually what people have learned. Typically, you would create a situation. Your audience brings that situation to life by acting out the words and actions of the characters in the role play. There are some considerations when using role playing in your training performance:

■ *Many people are intimidated by role playing.* They either sit on the sidelines and watch or are so nervous they can't effectively participate in the role play. One way to help is to conduct the role plays in small groups rather than in a large group. This lessens the personal risk to the audience member. Also, it may be a good idea to ask for volunteers rather than choosing people.

FYI...

A great twist on role playing is to videotape the role-plays. Use them as training opportunities with your audience.

- *Effective role playing requires trust.* Before an individual will feel comfortable playing out the scene, he or she needs to have some knowledge and trust of the people they are interacting with. Save your role-play activities for later in the session when the audience members have become familiar with each other.

Regardless of the game or activity, consider the amount of time it will take and how much time you have in the performance.

Audience Size

The size of your audience is a key consideration in the selection of games or activities. When possible, try to keep your class size to 25-30 people. In situations where numbers are high, consider two sessions of the class at different times. If that's not possible, you will need to decide what you can do in a larger group and how you can manage the game or activity in the training performance.

Opening and Closing the Session

You've written the main part of the script. You now have a good idea of what you are going to cover, how you are going to present it, the materials you are going to use and a plan for the measurement of learning. The next step is to plan how to open and close the performance. These two parts are critical to the success of the training performance.

People are more apt to remember the first and last things they hear and see.

Great Openings Include:

- Welcoming the group
- Introductions/Icebreaker
- Setting the norms
- Establishing the expectations
- Mapping out the agenda.

How you open the training performance will determine the tone for the rest of the day. How you close the performance will determine what people will take away with them. Planning for openings and closings rather than just letting them happen can eliminate stress and increase effectiveness.

The Opening

The opening should be designed to create a positive, casual environment, conducive to learning. It is during the opening of the session that you really have the opportunity to set the tone for the rest of the day.

Introductions/Icebreakers.

Creating a friendly, open environment begins with creating ways for the audience to get to know one another. Have the attendees introduce themselves. You can have them just give their name and their position or ask for additional specific information. You can ask them to tell you their favorite color, the first musical concert they ever went to, or even what their favorite hobby is. You can follow that up with another icebreaker or activity to get them working or communicating with one another.

> **Icebreakers**
> Icebreakers are activities designed to get things going. They typically involve the whole group and are usually short in length. They are used:
>
> - To help get the audience more comfortable
> - To introduce a topic
> - To help people get to know each other
> - At the beginning of a training session or module.[1]

Establish Norms

Norms are the behaviors or accepted practices everyone agrees to follow during the training performance. When training in today's environment, it's important to establish norms during your opening. It's also important everyone is in agreement on what the norms are. These norms help everyone understand what behavior is acceptable and unacceptable during the training performance. Norms also help you manage the training performance environment.

TRAINER TERMS

Norms –
   behaviors or accepted practices everyone agrees to follow during the training performance

An Example...

Have the audience brainstorm a list of norms they would like to see practiced throughout the training performance. As the audience makes suggestions write them on a flip chart, large enough for everyone to see. (You can ask an audience member to help out by writing on the flip chart for you.) Once the list is complete, it can be displayed all day. Some possible norms may include:

- Be on time (back from breaks and lunch)
- Everyone will participate
- Respect one another (appreciate that everyone is unique and brings different perspectives to the room)
- Have fun
- Ask questions.

Once the norms have been identified and listed, ask the audience: "Can everyone agree to live with these for the remainder of the class?" Typically, since they came up with them, everyone will agree. Once everyone has agreed to them, you can refer back to them throughout the performance, especially if someone is not behaving appropriately.

> FYI...
>
> Setting norms is a great way to manage the learning environment throughout the day. When an audience member is disrespectful, you can refer him or her back to the agreement.

Establish Expectations

Start by finding out what the audience expectations are for the class. What knowledge or information would they like to walk away with? There are no right or wrong answers. Once again, use a flip chart to create a master list of what the audience expects. At points throughout the day, you may want to refer to the list to ensure that you are meeting their needs.

An Example...

You are conducting a training performance on leadership. You ask your audience: "What are some topics you would like to see discussed today?"

Some examples of their answers may include:

■ Learn how to be a better listener

■ Learn more about dealing with conflict

■ Learn how to become a better mentor

■ Learn what tools the company has to help develop employees.

Keep in mind if you ask for this type information, you need to try to address the issues throughout the class. You should also be sure your learning objectives are incorporated in the list of expectations. In the closing session, you should summarize and make sure you were able to meet the expectations or be able to explain why not.

Rules for Asking Questions

In every training performance, audience members will have questions. To properly manage the environment and make it meaningful for everyone, it's important to set up some rules around asking questions. Can audience members ask questions anytime during the performance or would you prefer they hold their questions to the end of a session? By establishing rules up front, it helps the audience know what to do. It also allows them to ask questions more freely.

The Agenda

The last piece of the opening puzzle is to provide the audience with a performance agenda. This is a very important part of the opening. It lets the audience know what will be covered during the training performance. It helps them prepare for the training. Take the time to briefly review the agenda:

Explain how the training performance will run including:

■ Any housekeeping information about breaks (including where the restrooms are, and smoking policies)

■ Rules about cell phones (off), beepers (on vibrate)

■ Any other relevant information they may need.

Great openings get your audience prepared for the session and focused on the topic. They also encourage the audience to open their minds to new learning.

Closing the Session

People remember the first thing and last thing they experience in any given situation. Therefore, how you end the performance is just as important as how you opened it. Your ending should provide closure for your audience and help reinforce the key points. Your closing should incorporate several important parts.

Great Closing Sessions Include:
■ Next steps
■ Q & A
■ Review expectations
■ Evaluation
■ Celebration/Recognition
■ Closing activity.

■ Next Steps

You have finished your performance and presented all your information to your audience. Now is the time to let them know what they need to do next. This may include how to apply their learning back on the job, any follow-up they may expect, or any additional classes they may need to take in the future.

■ Schedule a Q & A Session

It's a good idea to allow time in your closing for a question and answer session. This allows an opportunity to gain closure for those audience members who have not asked questions previously. There may have been issues through the training they had a question about and didn't feel it was appropriate to interrupt the discussion to ask it. Some best practices around the Q & A session include:

■ Set a time limit.

■ Move closer to the audience.

■ If you don't know the answer, tell them you will get it for them.

■ Listen carefully for what question is really being asked.

■ Repeat or rephrase the question.

■ Don't evaluate the question (avoid saying "Good question!").

■ Keep your answers short and concise. The fastest way to shut down an audience is by taking 10 minutes to answer one question!

■ Warn the audience when you are wrapping up by saying: "One more question" or "Last question" so they know ahead of time you are finished.

- If you have hostile questioners:
  - Never argue
  - Find something to agree on
  - Don't use "but."
- Keep a list of the questions. If you are teaching the training performance again, you may want to incorporate some of the issues that came up in the Q & A session.

- Review Expectations

  Before wrapping up and moving into the audience evaluations, go back to the expectations list collected in the opening. Review the list to be sure the audience expectations have been met. If you have been keeping an eye on the list, you should have met their needs. Reviewing the list in the closing session helps reinforce what they have learned and completes the training loop.

- Evaluation

  Continuous improvement and audience feedback are the "Breakfast of Champions" for great performers. Every session you teach should include some way for your audience to evaluate your training. Chapter 11 will go into detail on types of evaluations and how to write them. Be sure you take the feedback in a constructive manner. When you ask for feedback, be prepared to accept it with a spirit of continuous improvement.

Some trainers will ask for feedback, then get defensive when an audience member disagrees with something he or she said or did. A better approach is to ask yourself the questions: "Why did they see it that way?" or "What are they seeing that I'm not?" These questions will help you see things from their perspective.

■ Celebration/Recognition

While this is not required, it is always a good idea to recognize your audience's attendance and participation. Some companies and trainers give certificates of completion or attendance for completed classes. Some give certificates of completion only after the participant can demonstrate the learned skills in the workplace. Regardless of what your company's practice is, it's important to recognize the contributions of the audience, even if it's just verbally!

Closing Activity

End your training on a light note by conducting a final closing activity. This gives your participants an opportunity to practice what they have learned or to end the day by just having fun!

WHEN YOU GET STUCK DURING SCRIPTING

There are times when it appears no matter how hard we try, we just have a "creativity block." You will know this is happening when one of the following occurs:

■ You can't think of an activity to include in a training class

■ You can't come up with a solution to a problem

■ You get frustrated trying to put together the project or training performance.

There are things you can do to break down these barriers. One of the most common strategies is to change activities for a while. Sometimes walking away for a few minutes or changing the "scenery" is just the break you need to get the creative juices flowing again. Other strategies include:

■ **Changing or Playing Music -** The type music you listen to can frequently get you thinking in a specific direction. If you get stuck, change the type of music to get you thinking differently or get the creativity flowing again!

■ **Adding Color to Your Environment -** Like music, color speaks to that part of your brain where creativity comes from. The next time you are having a creativity block, try using colored paper instead of white. Try using crayons, colored markers, or colored pencils to write with rather than the usual black or blue pen.

■ **Getting Rid of Interruptions -** No sooner does our mind get started but the phone rings. By the time you answer, take care of the issue, and get back to work, it's like starting all over again. The fewer the interruptions, the more you can get done.

REFERENCE

1.   Salopek, Jennifer. "Stop Playing Games." Training & Development. February, 1999. p. 34.

SKILL BUILDERS

Write a mini-lecture and then respond to the following questions.

1.   What will you do to engage your audience?

2.   What will you do to enhance the flow of performance?

3.   What would be the best setup for your training room?

4.   What activities would you include? How many will be independent and how many will be for the entire group?

5.   What A/V equipment would be required?

Chapter 7

DEVELOPING THE SCRIPT

PART 3: CREATING THE PROPS

Your words are the greatest power you have — Sonia Croquette

IN THIS CHAPTER:

- **The Audience Script**
- **The Actor's (Trainer's) Script**
- **Preparing to Use Technology**
- **Ethics in Training**
- **Reference**
- **Skill Builders**

The third part of script writing is to develop the additional materials you will need in your performance. In Part 2, you mapped out what activities to do to teach the materials. This chapter looks at ways to create your own materials for the performance and make your handouts, visuals, and workbooks shine.

At-a-Glance Guide to Script Writing

Part 3: Creating the Props – Chapter 7	
Audience Script (Participant's Handbook)	■ Develop training workbooks ■ Develop handouts and materials for the audience.
Develop Audio/Visual Aids	■ Develop any overheads, presentations, graphics, flip charts, etc., needed.
Actor's Script (Facilitator's Guide)	■ Create notes for the actor to follow during the performance ■ Incorporate references to visuals, activities, written materials, breaks, exercises, etc.
Be Ethical	■ Give credit where credit is due.

THE AUDIENCE SCRIPT

The audience script is much like a playbill. It is written to provide attendees with the key parts of the performance, a place to take notes, and worksheets for various activities such as handouts, case studies, or a participant handbook. When writing the audience script, you need to keep focused on providing them with a guide that meets **their** needs. You want to be sure to help them be organized for optimum learning.

Writing the Audience Script

The audience script is an important piece of the training performance. If materials are well written, professional, creative, and useful, it will enhance learning and ultimately help create a positive perception of the class. Be sure materials are professionally developed and well organized. If the materials are copies of copies that are hard to read, sloppy, and poorly written, this will negatively impact the audience's perception of the class. The more time and effort you spend developing the script, the greater the chance the training will have an impact on learning.

Relevant Content—The content of the audience script has to be useful and relevant. When researching and gathering information, it is easy to get sidetracked with interesting information that has no relevance to the learning objectives of the training performance. The audience has to be able to see how the information can be applied to their life or job. Be sure to link the relevance of information you provide to the topic and the audience. The best way to do this is to map all your content to your learning objectives.

Friendly and Easy to Read—The layout and design of the audience script must be **user friendly** and easy to read. You should create materials organized in such a way it is logical for the reader. When written materials are hard to use and information is difficult to find, the reader will often give up and not read it at all. Ultimately, this negatively impacts the learning experience. It is also important to make sure it's written at a level the learner can read.

TRAINER TERMS

User Friendly –
describes things that are easy for the user to access, read, use, and understand. They are well organized and appropriate for the level of the audience.

Avoid Big Words and Jargon—Be sure to avoid using words your audience may have trouble understanding. It is not your goal to impress them with the big words in your vocabulary. These will create roadblocks in the audience's ability to learn. Another challenge is industry-specific lingo, or jargon. Many industries have words, phrases, or acronyms that only make sense to that industry! While it's important to use language your audience understands, it's equally important for them to learn the language of the industry. If you use jargon, industry lingo, and acronyms, define the words for your audience. This will make it easier to learn.

Sometimes in an attempt to give complete information about a given topic, trainers will put everything in the manual. This confuses the reader. Be selective about content.

Chunk your Information—Take information and break it down into short, digestible pieces. People are no longer willing to sort through mountains of information. They want information that is well thought out and presented in "bite-sized" pieces. Chunking the information allows the audience to grasp it more easily. It boils paragraphs of text down to its bare essentials. The information can then be presented in bulleted points and short sentences. This process forces the author to be concise in presenting the information. You also want your materials to be a good reference tool when participants are back on the job.

> FYI...
>
> When information is chunked into smaller pieces, audience members will be able to refer back to the content easily. It's reusable!

Presenting Written Information—How you present written information determines whether people will read it or not. We have become a very visual society. We assign meaning and value based on how things look. When designing the audience script, create a layout that is useful and has "eye appeal." Remember who your audience is when designing materials for them.

> **Zemke, et. al., in the book *Generations @ Work*, suggests that:**
>
> ■ **The Veteran or Senior generation** prefers larger prints and simpler fonts. They like information well organized and supported with facts, figures, details, etc.
>
> ■ **The Boomer generation** wants training materials that are scannable and include a great deal of information.
>
> ■ **The Gen-Xers** prefer multiple graphics, words, etc., on the same page. They want lots of things on each page.
>
> ■ **The Nexters** read more than previous generations. They prefer an interactive format.[1]

Use Pictures—One way to add visual interest to your audience script is through the use of pictures. The old saying still works: "A picture is worth 1,000 words"! There are many different ways to enhance your script pictures, photos, graphics, and/or charts.

The Actor's (Trainer's) Script

It is important to understand that while the actor in the theater has only one script, the trainer has two parts to the script. The first part of the script is for the audience and the second part of the script is for the actor. The actor's script provides you with the guidelines you will use while delivering your content during the training performance. Examples of your script may include:

- A facilitator guide
- Class notes
- A/V presentations.

This script provides you with direction when communicating your message (training topic). It also serves to keep you focused. The actor's script outlines all the content, activities, notes, and additional information you want to deliver during the training performance. The more detailed the script, the better your performance will be. It is also important that the audience script be consistent with the actor's script. The content should be in the same order. All the information in the audience script should be used or at least referred to during the training performance.

Some tips for creating your script:

- Organize your material in the order you want to present it. Use your outline as your guide.
- Identify key concepts you want to reinforce.
- Take your organized content and put it into the format that will work best for you in the performance.
- Insert graphics, icons, or other distinguishing marks to help guide you through the script.
- Once you have your script, prepare any audio/visual presentations you want to accompany your performance.

Script Layout

Keeping track of all the elements of a performance can be challenging. It is important to have your script laid out in a way that is easy to follow. If you will be giving the performance, choose a layout that works for you. Some of the most popular ways of organizing actor scripts include:

- **Creating a checklist** - a list of topics to be covered
- **Spreadsheet or matrix format** - use a chart to track the flow of information
- **Outline form** - an outline with primary and secondary headings and information
- **Paragraph form** - notes are written in paragraphs, with a topic sentence and supporting sentences and examples
- **Individual note cards** - notes are written on individual cards, with each topic having its own card.
- **Sample wording** - the notes consist of short key words and phrases, organized so your eye can easily flow down the page and see key information at a glance.

There is no right or wrong way to lay out your script, only the best way for you to deliver the content. Keep in mind notes written in paragraph form can be more challenging to follow during the performance. You may want to highlight your key concepts so they don't get lost in all the text.

Windowpanes

If you are unsure of the flow of the content and want the overview of the training performance accessible during training, you may want to consider a matching windowpane.

TRAINER TERMS

Windowpane –
a term used in this context as a summary sheet for training. It often includes: topics, key points, length of time, goals, and content.

Windowpanes are also referred to as a "quick reference guide" or an "at-a-glance" sheet. One consolidates your entire outline to one sheet of paper by using only key words. It may also include tomfooleries for activities. Windowpanes provide you with a quick way to refocus if you lose your place.

An Example...

A windowpane for the employee turnover outline may look like this:

Main Topic	Key Points	Length of Time	Materials Needed	Additional Comments
Recruiting:	Hire the right employee	20 min	Facilitator guide Pages 1-6	
	Tools for recruiting	20 min	Role-play script	
	Role-play activity	10 min	Participant handbook pages 1-3	
	Recruitment strategies	20 min		
Training:	How training impacts employee satisfaction	10 min	Facilitator guide pages 7-12	
	Orientation training	20 min	Sample orientation handbook	
	Tools available for training	20 min		
	Training the trainer activity	30 min	Participant handbook pages 4-6	
	Strategies for providing consistent training for everyone	10 min		
Recognition:	Ways to recognize employees	30 min	Facilitator guide pages 13-16	
	Company-wide recognition programs	30 min	Participant handbook pages 7-10	

Using Graphics or Icons

To help keep you organized, you may want to include a few well-selected graphics to be used in your actor's (facilitator's) script for quick reference. Using icons (small pictures) in the margins of your actor's script can help you quickly scan your notes to see what is coming up next. For example, every time you want to place something on a flip chart, you may want to place a flip chart graphic in the margin.

 Use flip chart   **Encourage students to take notes**   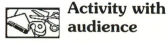 **Activity with audience**

Trainers will often say, "Oh, I'll remember that! I don't have to write it down!" The reality is that in the heat of the moment (during the training performance), there are many things going on and facilitators often forget things. The best thing to do is write everything down. If you don't need it, great, but if you do need it, it's there!

Outside Facilitators

There may be times when you are developing the training but others will be delivering the content. If this is the case, the actor's script will need to be more detailed and provide very specific instructions. Things to consider when designing the script for outside facilitators include:

- The facilitator may be a content expert but may need your help to organize the delivery of the information.

- The facilitator may be a great trainer but may not have your content expertise. You will need to provide him or her with very detailed content information in this case.

- The facilitator may be teaching for the very first time and have no experience. In this situation, you may have to provide training on how to deliver the information as well as the information itself.

Learner-Centered Approach

Regardless of who is conducting the program, a learner-centered approach must be taken. In other words, be creative in trying to engage your audience. Be sure to include activities that involve the whole person: the mind, body, and spirit of the person.

Preparing to Use Technology

While writing your script, you need to consider what A/V aids you will use. Each piece of equipment has different advantages. The following are some basic guidelines to keep in mind while writing your script:

Flip Charts

Guidelines for flip charts include:

- Plan ahead: Think before you start writing.
- Include no more than three points per page.
- Use markers that are sharp and colors that are not washed out.
- Use a maximum of three colors on a page.
- Use colors that are difficult to see as accent colors only. Some of these include red, pink, yellow, light or lime green, and orange.
- Draw graphics or designs that help make your flip charts look interesting.
- Prepare your flip charts before class.
- Practice with them.

To make your flip chart presentations more professional, follow these helpful tips:

- Use flip chart paper that has grid lines. This helps keep your printing straight, and the audience can't see the grids from their seats.
- Post-It® Flip Charts are great for hanging around the room (provided the wall surface is cooperative!) Just like the small Post-It® notes, they have an adhesive strip on the back.
- Use a pencil to write notes in margins. It's a great way for you to remember key points associated with the flip chart.

PowerPoint® or Overhead Transparency Slides

When creating screens, slides, sheets, or pages for PowerPoint® presentations and overhead transparencies, keep in mind the following:

- Have no more than one key concept or main idea per slide
- Have some white space (in other words, don't fill up every inch of the slide)
- Use bulleted lists, not a paragraph format
- Use pictures and graphics
- Have no more than six lines per slide
- Use no more than three colors per slide
- Be visual, creative, and use graphics, but don't overdo it and create clutter!

FYI...

When creating PowerPoint® presentations consider the following:

- Ask yourself: Can this concept be conveyed by an image? A flow chart? A graph?
- On text: Use bullets, delete unnecessary words.
- Put words in different visual formats: vary fonts, colors, and sizes.
- Use different text box shapes.
- Vary slide layout.
- Add art, graphics, and pictures.

Videos

Video segments can add interest to a presentation. Be sure to introduce and explain the purpose of the video and how it will apply to the audience. Watch the entire video prior to the training session. Write down exactly which parts you are going to use. Be sure to identify the concepts you want the video to reinforce.

Long video segments can be ineffective if they allow a viewer to settle into a TV-watching mode. Consider breaking videos over 20 minutes long into multiple parts.

ETHICS IN TRAINING

One last topic that needs to be considered when "writing the script" is ethics. In the materials we use and the discussions we undertake with our audiences, we need to understand our ethical responsibility. This responsibility extends both in and out of the training performance. It includes personal integrity to the authors and publishers of the materials we use.

Don't use someone else's words and call them your own. Don't take someone else's materials and claim them as yours. Follow the copyright laws and the trademark restrictions. Remember, the best way to teach others to be ethical is to set the standard and be a role model for the behavior you want others to follow.

Benchmarking, **copyrights**, and **registered trademarks** are common terms to anyone who creates, writes, or performs. They are also terms every ethical trainer needs to understand.

FYI...

Original works created on or after January 1, 1978, are protected by copyright law for the author's life plus 70 years after his/her death.

TRAINER TERMS

Copyright – means the author or publisher has exclusive rights to a piece of information, a book, or other materials. If you want to use information from copyrighted material, you must receive permission from the author or publisher.

Registered Trademark – means the person or company has registered a name, phrase, brand, or item, and has exclusive rights to that name, phrase, brand, or item.

REFERENCE

1. Zemke, Ron. *Generations @ Work*. AMACOM. New York. 2000.

SKILL BUILDERS

1. What are the differences between the actor's script and the audience's script?

2.   Create props to support a mini-lecture. Each prop should be independent and linked to the mini-lecture.

3.   Develop the actor's script to support a mini-lecture. Be sure to include references to visuals, activities, written materials, breaks, and exercises.

Chapter 8

SETTING THE STAGE

Learning is enhanced when participants' physical and psychological comfort is considered. — Coleman Lee Finkel

IN THIS CHAPTER:

- **Scheduling the Performance**
- **Selecting the Stage**
- **The Training Room (Your Stage)**
- **Stage Setup (Room Setup)**
- **Designing Marketing Materials for Your Training**
- **Audience Logistics**
- **Contracts**
- **Tracking Attendance**
- **Skill Builders**

SCHEDULING THE PERFORMANCE

You have written a great script and it's time to bring it to life! Creating an environment conducive to learning is a major contributor to your success. The physical environment, or your stage, is the foundation for everything else. Planning the location, logistics, and the procedures involving audience attendance are important pieces in setting your stage.

Choosing a Date

Choosing a date for the training performance can be one of the most difficult jobs in setting your stage. There is never going to be a perfect date when you are dealing with many people across several departments. Consider dates that are best for the majority of the audience members. Check if any company-wide initiatives are scheduled on the proposed date that would negatively impact the attendance of the training performance. Consider events outside the workplace that might also negatively impact attendance. Now, choose your date. You may want to have one primary date and several backup dates that can be used if needed.

> **FYI...**
> Keep in mind if you have a mandatory class and a large number of participants, you may want to schedule several sessions of the class at different times or on different days. This ensures you will have the class size you want, and it helps your audience have flexibility with their schedule.

SELECTING THE STAGE

Just as choosing the right theater can enhance a theatrical performance, choosing the right training room can play a key role in the success of the training performance. For some, training will be held **in-house**, or in meeting space within the company's facility. For others, training may need to be held in a rented or contracted space.

T R A I N E R   T E R M S

In-house –
   term used to refer to training conducted in a training room or classroom located within the company's building or site.

Some locations you have to choose from include:

- Restaurant banquet space
- Hotel meeting rooms or banquet rooms
- Conference centers
- Catering halls
- Local university or school facilities
- Retreat centers.

Some locations you may want to avoid include:

- Cafeterias
- Non-classroom settings
- Locations having multiple activities occurring simultaneously
- Locations that require significant travel time.

There are many factors that determine the selection of your training performance space or your "stage." The physical location of the space, the features, services, equipment, and costs all contribute to the selection process.

The Facility's Location

The location of the facility may drive your decision. Location can be even more critical if transportation of a group is involved. You may also need to consider whether or not attendees will need to return to work following the training performance. Some questions to consider when choosing a location include:

- Is it accessible and easy to get to?
- Will the audience be able to find it?
- Is there transportation available to the site?
- Is there parking available?

Type of Facility

The type of facility may also play a key role in your decision. The most beautiful setting in the world won't work if it doesn't fit your needs. You may need to check the facility for size, the availability of A/V equipment, and the ability to serve meals if needed.

Often trainers will like the way a certain room looks and choose it even if it may be a "little crowded" when the audience arrives. Feeling closed in or uncomfortably close to others has a negative impact on learning. Make sure your room has ample space.

THE TRAINING ROOM (YOUR STAGE)

Now that you are considering a specific location, you need to complete a thorough inspection of the actual room, or stage, where you will be performing. Things you should be checking include:

- Capacity
- Layout
- Color
- Decor
- Lighting
- Support for your A/V needs.

Stage Capacity

Capacity is a very important consideration for a number of reasons. There are several variables that can affect the number of people a room can hold including:

- The setup of the room
- The type of A/V equipment needed
- The number of extra tables required
- The type of activities you will be conducting throughout the training performance.

You want your audience to feel comfortable and able to learn. There has to be ample space for them to move around. A cramped room inhibits learning. It shortens attention span and hampers creativity. It also limits your ability to conduct activities and group projects.

TRAINER TERMS

Room Capacity –
the number of people a room can hold. Capacity will vary based on table setup, A/V requirements, planned activities or other reasons.

Stage Layout

Often in banquet halls or hotel meeting rooms, there are pillars that block people's ability to see the entire presentation. Odd-sized rooms, such as a long narrow room, will limit how you can organize the seating arrangements of the audience. Additionally, audience members in the back of the room may have a more difficult time hearing and seeing what's going on in the training performance. Expect these attendees to become frustrated and you will lose their attention.

Stage Color

A great deal of research has been done on the role colors and textures play in learning. Some research results for wall colors include:

- Soft blues, greens, and neutral colors have been identified as best for enhancing learning by easing strain on the eyes and by creating a calming effect.
- Busy patterns should be avoided. If conducting a one-day or multiple-day training performance, busy or loud patterns can actually interfere with the learning process.
- Room size plays a role on colors and patterns as well. Small rooms should be done in lighter colors, with little or no patterns. You have more freedom in larger rooms.

Many trainers think the walls in a training room should be painted white. White is actually too bright and, depending on lighting, can actually strain the audience's eyes. Neutral or soft colors are a better choice.

Stage Decor

How the room is decorated can also impact learning. Too many decorations can be very distracting and cause the audience to get agitated. The number and size of the decorations can also cause the room to feel smaller. This may cause the audience to feel that the room is "closing in" on them. Decor should be simple, appropriate and conducive to learning.

Stage Lighting

There are several challenges with lighting. First of all, it's not only important to have sufficient lighting, but it is also important to have the right kind of lighting. Frequently, rooms like hotel banquet rooms have lighting not conducive to learning. The lighting may be too dark or too harsh. The best type lighting is a soft white. It also needs to be bright enough for the audience to read, take notes, and see materials.

FYI...

One of the challenges in training rooms today is the lighting scheme when using technology. Actors using PowerPoint® presentations in their training performance often turn the lights down so the audience can see the slides. Unfortunately, this places a strain on the audience's eyes, especially if they are trying to take notes in this darker environment.

Stage Setup (Room Setup)

The facility and room have been decided on. The next decision to make is how you want the room to be set up for the training performance. Depending on the facility, your choices may be numerous or limited. Entire books have been written on this topic. In this section of the chapter, we will discuss some of the more common room setups.

Table Types

There are several different types of tables you can choose in room setup. They include:

> **FYI...**
> Every person has an individual comfort zone with respect to physical distance from others. The comfort zone or distance for social or workplace interactions is 3 to 7 feet. Keep this in mind when designing the layout of your room. Additionally, these distances may vary from country to country.

- **Classroom-style tables**—typically 4 feet long by 18 inches wide. These are used primarily for classroom-style setup.

- **Banquet tables**—6 feet long by 30 inches wide. These are used primarily for U-shaped or square-shaped setups. They are also used for buffets, breaks, and sometimes to display training materials.

- **Round tables**—come in a variety of sizes. The most common sizes are 60 inches, 72 inches and 90 inches. The primary difference of these tables is how many will sit comfortably around them. When using these for the training performance, consider placing fewer people around the table than you normally would.

Setup Types

There are several different room setup variations to choose from. The more common ones include:

■ **Theater Style**

This style does not include tables. Chairs are placed in rows, all facing the front, with an aisle in the center. The actor is in the front of the room. This setup can handle large numbers of people and is fine for short presentations. However, there are problems with this setup including:

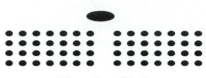

Theater Style

- ■ The challenge of attendees taking notes and trying to balance everything simultaneously

- ■ Attendees organizing personal belongings placed on the floor or under the audience member's feet, while they are trying not to step on them or kick them.

■ **Classroom or Schoolroom Style**

This style is set up using classroom-style tables set in rows. Chairs are placed on one side of the table facing forward. The actor is usually at the front of the room. This style takes up a great deal of space. It can also accommodate large groups, but often the audience members in the back have trouble seeing any audio/visual being used. There are several versions of this setup including:

- ■ Open – Two rows of tables with an aisle down the center
- ■ Closed – Two to three tables set together in a row with aisles on either side
- ■ V-shaped – Tables are set up like the open style but angle toward the front with an aisle down the center.

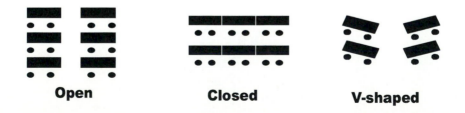

Open   **Closed**   **V-shaped**

■ U-shape

The U-shape is very good for a small number of people. This setup uses three banquet tables set in the shape of a U. Chairs are placed around the outside of the U, facing into the center. The actor stands at the open end of the U. The disadvantages of this room setup include:

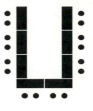

U-shape

- It is not conducive to small group activities
- The U-shape requires a great deal of room.

■ Square

The square setup uses banquet tables like the U-shape but is set in the shape of a square. Chairs are set up around the outside perimeter of the square, facing the center. Typically the actor is sitting with the audience members. The biggest disadvantage to this setup is the difficulty in using audio/visual equipment. This setup is used for small groups, 16 people or less. It is good for:

Square

- Group discussion
- Conveying a sense of equality.

■ Rounds

Using round tables in the training room can be very effective in facilitating small group discussions. Depending on the size of the table (60", 72", 90") you can sit four to eight people per table. You should try to put fewer people at a table for training than you would for other activities. You may only want to place chairs around half the table (sometimes referred to as a crescent setup) so everyone is facing toward the front of the room. The benefits of round tables include:

- Facilitating discussion between audience members
- Ease of group activities
- Allowing the actor to move around the room.

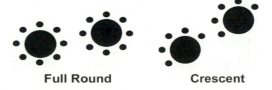

Full Round   **Crescent**

Type of Setup	Group Size	Advantages	Disadvantages
Theater Style	Large Groups	Easy setup	Difficult for attendees taking notes.
Classroom Style	Large Groups	Many varieties	Takes up large amount of space.
U-shape	Small Groups	Intimate setting	Difficult for small group activities.
Square	Small Groups	Good for group discussion	Difficult to use most A/V equipment.
Rounds	Medium Groups	Facilitates small group discussions	Takes up large amount of space.

Audio/Visual Needs

Selecting your audio/visual equipment is a critical step in setting your stage. If you are unsure of your A/V requirements, reserve all pieces of equipment you think you might need. You can always add or cancel equipment before the event. Just make sure any changes you make or additional equipment you request is done in ample time to ensure you can get it. If you are using your own A/V equipment, ensure that it is in good working order.

FYI...

When reserving space and equipment, ask the sales person or representative how many days prior to the event can you still request or cancel A/V.

Some of the more common A/V equipment includes:

- **Flip Charts**—Easels with large pads of paper on them. They are still widely used and play a key role in many training performances. Flip charts should be placed where all audience members can see and use them.

- **White Board or Dry Erase Board**—Uses dry erase markers. In rooms where these are permanently installed, they can double as a projector screen if needed. They are great for writing down thoughts that occur during training and are easy to erase.

- **Overhead Projector with Screen**—This piece of equipment uses transparencies projected to a large white screen or wall. Prior to the popularity of LCD projectors, overhead projectors were a very common component of training. They are still a great backup when technology breaks down or to provide variety in your presentation. Many trainers use them when information is being addressed that the audience needs constant access to.

- **TV/VCR**—Televisions come in a variety of sizes. The larger the group, the larger the screen required. For groups over 100, you may want to consider several monitors placed around the room and cabled together.

- **Video Camera**—Allows you to videotape role-plays in the training session. When using these, make sure you provide each member of the audience with his or her own videotape. It's also a good idea to allow them to keep their tape after the training performance. If you intend to use the audience videotapes in future training performances, be sure to have them sign a release.

- **LCD Projector with Screen**—A projector that takes the image from your computer and projects it on to a large white screen. There are three fairly common types:
    - Projectors that sit on a table or cart in front of the screen.
    - Projectors that are permanently fixed in a given location, usually hanging from the ceiling with a remote connection.
    - Rear screen projectors designed for larger presentations. These are located behind the screen.

- **Electronic White Boards**—Like a standard white board, but connected to a computer. You can record all the notes written on the board. There are also interactive white boards which display your computer desktop. The board acts as a touch screen where you can open applications, navigate websites, and write and save hardboard notes.

- **Laser Pointer**—A pencil-sized, battery-operated device that projects a red beam and is used to point out various highlights on a large projector screen.

- **CD Player**—Used to play musical CDs. In larger facilities, these are connected to the audio system and piped into the room. In smaller, less sophisticated facilities, they may be stand-alone players with individual speakers.

- **Digital Cameras**—Cameras that capture and store still images as digital data instead of on film. The rapid transfer of data to computer stations allows for nearly immediate use of images.

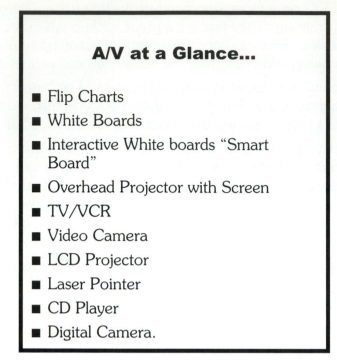

Technology

In addition to more traditional A/V needs, today's training environment may require computer labs that can run simulation exercises, have Internet connections, and are capable of video conferencing. These more advanced training aids may require a technician to assist in setting up and possibly to run the equipment during the training performance.

Food and Beverage

Another key consideration in setting the stage is creating a sense of hospitality. One way to embody the spirit of hospitality is by providing refreshments. At a minimum, you should always provide beverages (even if it's just water). Providing breakfast, mid-morning snacks, lunch, and afternoon breaks can be an important part of training as well.

TRAINER TERMS

F&B –
   common acronym used to refer to food and beverage. It is often used in hotels and convention centers when discussing meals and events related to meetings.

■ **Breakfast –** This doesn't have to be elaborate. It can be yogurt, bagels, fresh fruit, coffee and juice, or a combination thereof.

■ **Breaks –** Snacks, candy, and cookies are more traditional break items and are still very popular. There is a trend, however, for healthier breaks. These breaks can include yogurt, water and juices, Power Bars®, granola bars, and other healthy snacks.

> **FYI...**
> Eating foods high in sugar gives people quick energy bursts and harsh energy drops within 20 minutes. If you want your learners to sleep after lunch, serve high carbohydrate meals such as pasta or potatoes.

■ **Lunch –** When planning meals, keep in mind the types food you choose can impact learning. Heavy foods may cause the performance to slow for a period of time in the afternoon. Studies also suggest turkey will relax audience members and sometimes make them drowsy. Additionally, you should always have a vegetarian alternative available. There may be other special dietary requirements that need to be considered. You may want to send out a questionnaire before the training performance inquiring about dietary needs.

What should you do if your budget does not include enough money for food and beverages? Consider less expensive alternatives such as bringing in chips or pretzels. Be sure to check with the facility on their policies for allowing food or beverage to be brought into the facility.

DESIGNING MARKETING MATERIALS FOR YOUR TRAINING

Think about what helps you decide on a theatrical performance to see. The storyline is one reason, but another is how well they marketed the show to you!

You can use some of the same strategies in your training performance marketing plan as they do in theatrical performance marketing plans.

Your basic marketing plan should include the following:

1. **Identify who your potential audience is**. Just as you did in writing your script, look at the demographics of the audience and their experience levels. Identify which methods of communication will work best.

2. **Select the methods of communication you will use** to market your class to potential audience members.

3. **Plan out what you want to say**. What are the "sound bites" or short messages you want the potential audience members to hear? Some basic elements that should be a part of your marketing plan include:

   - An explanation of the training performance or storyline.
   - A description of what's in it for the attendee.
   - Highlighted special components of the training performance that might interest potential audience members and encourage them to come.
   - Specific performance details including the day, the date, and the time it is being held.
   - Location highlights including where it's being held and information on any transportation being provided (if applicable).
   - The signup cutoff date.
   - A contact name and phone number if they should have any questions.
   - An enrollment form or instructions on how to sign up for the performance. Note: when designing your enrollment form ask the potential audience member to include any:
     - Special physical requirements
     - Special dietary requirements
     - Special learning requirements.
   - The marketing pieces (flyers, e-mail messages). Be creative! Use action words. Make the announcement sizzle!

4. **Determine the dates for distribution**. How soon prior to the training performance do you want to start marketing it? If you are using several

methods, how much time do you want between communications? It's important to send information out early enough so attendees can schedule for it. Be careful though; you don't want to send it out so early people forget about it by the time the performance takes place. You may want to send some general announcements out earlier, letting potential audience members know the training performance is coming. Follow up several weeks later with a more detailed informational piece.

5. **Consider payments for training**. Will there be a cost for the class? If so, how will you be receiving payment? Is it possible to transfer funds internally? Will someone need to approve payments? If so, who would that be and what type of process will you need to put into place to make sure it happens?

6. **Establish rules around RSVPs and the registration process**. Options include having potential audience members:

   ■ Complete a registration form and return it by a certain date

   ■ Send an RSVP via e-mail

   ■ Go to the company intranet site and register on-line

   ■ Call a phone number that has been set up for the purpose of registering for a class

   ■ Talk to their managers and have them sign the individual up for the class

   ■ Come the day of the training performance.

7. **Stick to the registration dates you have set.** If you start making too many exceptions in the registration process, you are setting yourself up for chaos. People will get the idea very quickly that it's OK to sign up late all the time. This makes it very difficult for you to plan correctly. If you stick to your deadlines, people will respect them and follow them in the future.

Marketing Hints:

■ **Use color and creative fonts**

■ **Use graphics and photographs when possible**

■ **Use expressive words and language when creating the announcement**

■ **Use unique techniques for getting the word out.**

Many trainers do not take the time and effort to create an announcement that accurately reflects the goals of the training performance. People reading the announcement may choose not to come because it doesn't look interesting. The key is to market the training performance with the same excitement you will use in delivering it!

AUDIENCE LOGISTICS

So far we have dealt with the physical environment and the details around the training performance. Another major part of setting the stage involves the logistics of the entire registration process. This includes everything from notifying the audience of the event to tracking their participation.

Notifying the Audience

You have several choices when it comes to notifying the audience of the training performance. You must first know whether the event is mandatory or elective. A mandatory class may only require a simple notice of the place and time of the performance. An elective training session may require a more creative marketing approach. In this case, you may want to consider multiple ways of sharing the event details with potential audience members.

Some ways or methods you can use to notify the audience include:

■ **Invitations**
This method requires you to send an invitation to each potential audience member. The invitations should list relevant information like where the event is, when it will be (both date and time), and some of the details of the training performance. This is a more formal method and implies they have a choice. This would not be recommended for a mandatory training performance.

■ **Announcements**

This method is a less personal way of letting everyone know this training performance is being held. It is a great way to introduce the training performance and can be very informative. Announcements can be used to introduce the training performance and to create a level of awareness. It would then need to be followed up with another method. Announcements are a good method to use for mandatory training.

■ **E-mail**

E-mail is a fast, effective way to reach all potential audience members. It can also be an efficient way to get responses by suggesting the audience member RSVP via e-mail. It's a great method for mandatory classes, provided all potential audience members have e-mail accounts or addresses. The downside of using this method is sometimes it can be challenging to be creative. It is not easy to create an e-mail message that will stand out in the receiver's mind. Again, this would be a great method, if used in conjunction with another method.

> FYI...
>
> If the class is not mandatory, you should contact the supervisors and let them know the class is being offered! If you have their support, you will usually have better attendance at your training performances.

■ **Flyers/Posters**

These are great tools for announcing an upcoming event. They also serve as a reinforcement tool or reminder to potential audience members. Flyers and posters allow you creativity and are very inexpensive. Additionally, they can be hung in a variety of locations throughout the workplace to constantly reinforce your message.

■ **Memos**

Memos are a more traditional method of informing potential audience members of upcoming events. Memos do not allow for as much creativity as other methods. However, if your company uses this method of communicating, then it may be an effective way to announce your training performance. It allows you to set a more formal tone.

Notifying the Audience Should Create Excitement

The key to any type of communication about the training performance is to create interest and excitement about it. The audience should want to attend whether it's mandatory or elective. They should be looking forward to the event, not dreading it. You can help create excitement through the methods discussed previously and through the way you market the performance. Take the same amount of time marketing the performance to your "in-house" customers that you would if you were marketing the class to external customers. Seeing the announcement in different ways helps create excitement as well.

CONTRACTS

Now that you have identified the training performance location, chosen the stage setup, and selected the food and beverage for the event, the next step is to finalize the deal. If you are going to be training at an off-site location, contact the sales representative and review your requirements with them. Once an agreement has been reached, they will send you a standard contract to sign. Make sure you read the contract before you sign it. Verify everything in the contract is exactly what was discussed and agreed to by both parties. You should pay particular attention to the following items:

- **Cancellation policy**
  Many contracts require a certain number of days prior to the event for cancellation. Once past that date, there may be a fee for cancellation.

- **Room rental costs**
  Make sure you review what is included with the room rental and what items are considered additional costs. For example, in some training facilities only the initial setup of the room is included. Any changes you may require to the room are an extra charge.

- **Room rental discounts**
  A common practice is to discount the cost of the room rental when ordering food and beverage. Review discounts carefully and take advantage of as many as possible.

- **Final count date**
  Often, when reserving the training room, you don't know exactly how many people will be attending the training performance. Most facilities require you to provide them with a final count or final number of people that will be attending the event several days prior to the performance. This is referred to as the number guaranteed. The **number guaranteed** is the number you will be charged for (with regard to food and beverage or other charges) regardless

of the number of audience members that actually attend the class. If the number of attendees is higher than the number guaranteed, and the facility was able to provide service for them, you will be charged for the

TRAINER TERMS

Number guaranteed –
a final count or final number of people that will be attending the event

additional people. Some facilities require you to have a minimum number of people guaranteed to receive certain discounts. They may even charge a penalty fee for having less than the guaranteed number.

■ **Additional fees**
Review the contract for clauses that list additional fees including costs for table linens, platforms, additional tables, room setup changes, or A/V setup.

Once you have read the contract, you should contact your sales representative to answer any questions you may have. In the long run, this could save you time, money, and frustration.

Frequently, trainers will accept things in the contract they disagree with because they don't want to cause conflict or "ruffle any feathers." It is your right as the renter, or customer, to negotiate or at the very least question items in the contract you don't agree with or understand.

TRACKING ATTENDANCE

Once you have identified how you will notify potential audience members, the next step is to decide how to track their attendance. You will have to track both the RSVP phase and the actual attendance phase.

■ Type the list of potential audience members.

■ Mark the date when they sent back their RSVP.

■ Take attendance the day of the performance and mark their attendance on the same sheet. Note: Keeping information all together and in one place saves time and makes it easier in the future.

Registration Process

Once you have identified how potential audience members will RSVP, you will need to determine how to capture the information you are receiving. You will also want to set up a method of communicating with your audience members prior to class. You may need to send them additional information about the class prior to the session. The process needs to be effective enough so everyone gets contacted.

When a class is mandatory, some actors believe it's not necessary to have the audience members sign up. This can cause significant problems in communication as well as tracking and follow-up. The key to keeping organized is to require everyone to RSVP.

Master List

It is important to maintain a master list of everyone who is attending the performance. The list of audience members should be put into a spreadsheet format. This spreadsheet should include relevant information about the audience members and activities related to them. This master list is what will be used from this point forward to manage the logistics of audience. The attendees on this list will become the "guaranteed" number of audience members attending the training performance. Your master list will be used for several other reasons:

■ It can be used to track the various activities around the training performance

■ It can help track what members have been contacted and verify they have been signed up for the class

- It can be used to track pre-work assignments and who has or hasn't returned the required assignments
- It can be used to track post-work assignment completion
- It can be used to prepare certificates of completion, name tags, and/or table tents.

You must stay organized and keep all the information in one place.

Many trainers don't take the time to maintain a master list. Then, on the actual day of the event, they are scrambling for information. Take the time during planning in order to set the performance up for success.

An Example... Registration Spreadsheet

Name	Date of Registration	Special Require-ments	Date Pre-work Sent	Date Pre-work Returned	Reminder Sent
Betsy Billboard	January 17	None	February 1	February 24	Yes
Sam Soup	January 14	Vegetarian	February 1	February 28	Yes
Mary Montana	January 12	None	February 1	February 28	Yes
Dave Door	January 16	Wheelchair access	February 1	February 20	Yes

Post-Performance Responsibility

Many actors believe once the performance is over, so is their responsibility. Great actors understand there are post-performance logistical responsibilities that help close the learning loop. These responsibilities may include:

- Tracking post-work requirement completions.
- Entering attendees into a database that tracks the classes they have attended. This may be required for various company career paths or manpower planning recommendations.
- Providing attendees with requirements of follow-up classes.
- Communicating with the audience members' supervisors or managers on any post-work requirements their employees may have as a result of the class.

Setting the stage takes a great deal of time and effort. Plan properly and do not take shortcuts; this will help to ensure a successful performance.

SKILL BUILDERS

1.   Create a list of considerations to be made when scheduling training.

2.   Review existing training and lay out the training room. Identify additional needs for A/V.

3.   Develop a marketing plan for a training performance. Include a calendar of events, distribution, and signup strategies.

4.   Develop a contract bid for a full-day performance that will be held at a local facility (hotel). Include food and beverage, room rental, and A/V logistics in the bid.

Chapter 9

DRESS REHEARSAL

By failing to prepare, you are preparing to fail. — Benjamin Franklin

IN THIS CHAPTER:

- **Getting Yourself Ready to Perform**
- **Manage the Environment**
- **Performance Day**
- **Co-performing**
- **Skill Builders**

GETTING YOURSELF READY TO PERFORM

In a theatrical performance, the actors have many rehearsals. As the actual event draws near, they have a dress rehearsal. The stage is set. The props are used. The actors are in costume. They rehearse the entire performance as if it were live in front of an audience.

In a training performance, a dress rehearsal also plays a key role in personally preparing the actor for the training performance. This dress rehearsal takes place at two different times: the days prior to the performance and the day of the performance.

Personal Preparation

Great actors, in their most memorable theatrical performances, attribute all their success to their preparation for the part and to continuous, concentrated rehearsals. Just as in any theatrical performance, personal preparation and rehearsal are the keys to any successful training performance. Unfortunately, it is the one thing most often skipped.

The perceived lack of time or an attitude of "I know this stuff, I don't have to prepare," are usually the reasons why people don't prepare. In reality, the better the preparation, the better the training performance. There are mental and physical components to your dress rehearsal. Each requires different activities, and both are equally important to the overall training performance.

Mental Preparation

The basic premise here is to prepare yourself mentally so you can create the best possible experience for your audience. There are several mental exercises that can help you get started:

1. Think about the best presenter you have ever seen.

   a. What made him or her good?

   b. What made him or her stand out in your mind?

2. Now think about the worst presenter you have ever seen.

   a. What made him or her the worst?

   b. What specific actions or behaviors made him or her poor?

   c. What could have made him or her better?

3. What are the best and worst learning environments you have been in?

   a. Was it the physical environment?

   b. Was the climate conducive to learning?

   c. Was there anything that really stuck out in your mind?

4. How can you use these experiences to make your training performance the best it's ever been?

   a. What techniques would you want to incorporate into your training?

   b. What things would you absolutely not want to do?

Why Are They Here?

A helpful step in mental preparation for your training performance is to understand why your audience is coming and what they will be expecting. How can you stand out and be respected? How are you going to make it a memorable experience?

To try to get a better understanding of why your audience will be coming to class, ask yourself the following questions about your performance:

1. Is it a requirement?

2. Is it voluntary?

3. Is it related to a company or process change?

4. Is it to learn a new task?

5. Is it for continuous learning and development?

As the facilitator, or actor, it is your responsibility to get excited about what you are going to teach. Focus on how your audience can grow from the experience.

Often trainers go into a training performance with the mindset that they are going to simply teach someone a new skill. Your role is more important. You are teaching a new skill or process but you are also offering your audience a memorable learning experience. You are creating an opportunity for them to grow both professionally and personally.

Visualize the Training Performance

Now that you are mentally aware of why your audience is attending the performance, your next step is visualization. Visualizing is an exercise that allows you mentally to draw a picture of how you want the performance to look, feel, and sound to your audience. Once you have visualized the performance, you will be able to take the steps necessary to bring it to life.

Try this visualization exercise:

Find a quiet place and bring along a pen and paper for taking notes. Ask yourself these questions and write down the answers:

1. What will the room look like?

    a.   What will be on the walls?

    b.   What will be on the tables?

    c.   What equipment will be in the room?

    d.   How will the room be set?

2. What will your performance sound like?

    a.   Will there be music?

    b.   Will people be talking to one another?

3. Where will you be standing?

    a. Are you in the front of the room?

    b. Are you moving around?

4. Where will your audience be?

    a. Will they be up close or far away?

    b. Will they be in groups?

5. What is your content?

    a. What is the sequence of events?

    b. What activities are you planning?

    c. How will you be testing?

6. Now visualize success. What would make this experience feel successful to you?

    a. Is it people asking questions?

    b. Is it when your audience gives you positive feedback?

    c. Is it when your audience can demonstrate the skill?

7. What would you want them to say about the class when they return to their work environment?

Try to be very detailed during this process. The more details you can visualize, the greater your chance for success. The saying goes… "if you don't know where you are going, any road will get you there!" It's easy to design the performance if you know what you want. If you don't know what you want, you can't set yourself up for success.

Anticipate Audience Questions

You also need to visualize the needs of the audience. Try to foresee the questions they may have. Put yourself in your audience's shoes. Write down questions you think they might ask. There are many ways to help you anticipate potential questions.

> **FYI…**
>
> **When conducting the performance, take note of questions being asked. These questions can help you uncover content design flaws that can be corrected for the next class!**

- If you have taught with this script before, what questions were asked then?

- When you were designing the content, what areas or topics were more difficult for you?

- What's the experiential level of the audience? The less experienced members may have content-related questions whereas the more experienced members may have application-related questions.

Take the time to answer the questions you have come up with. Working through this process will help you provide better answers to audience questions while building your confidence in answering their questions.

Prepare Yourself Physically

The mental preparation is complete; now it is time to prepare physically. Once the registration process is complete; you will want to contact the attendees one more time. This should take place a week or two before the actual training performance. You could do this via e-mail, by phone, or a post card. This will show the attendees you are prepared and the training performance is important to you.

Your communication should include a brief overview of what they can expect during the performance. This will allow *the attendees* to come as mentally prepared as you do. This also gives you the opportunity to uncover any "hot buttons" or issues prior to training. When you contact them, be sure to provide them with the goals of the session and the agenda. You should also ask them to contact you with any issues or concerns about the performance. You may also want to contact their supervisors to find out if there are any specific issues they feel you should address on the topic.

Additional Materials

You can't always completely predict how a performance is going to go. You may have an audience of **fast track learners** who are flying through your content. You may want to challenge them with additional information. On the other hand, you may have a group of learners who are being exposed to the storyline for the first time and require additional exercises or activities to fully understand

TRAINER TERMS

Fast Track Learners –
people who learn things very quickly and want to move on to the next topic just as quickly

the topic. When preparing for the performance, create a few additional activities and some additional information related to your topic. You may not need it, but if you do, you'll have it!

Go Shopping

You may want to purchase some inexpensive prizes or candy that can be passed out as rewards during the training performance. Even if you are not planning a reward system, prepare for it rather than try to pull something together at the last minute. It can be helpful to use your shopping trip as mental preparation time.

Create a Checklist for Materials

Make a checklist of materials, props, supplies, training aids, and other items you will use for the training performance. Include anything you will need to facilitate the training: any audience member handouts, game materials and supplies, and any recognition prizes.

Props and Training Aids	Training Supplies
Make sure you have all your performance props and training aids ready for your training. Don't assume everything is there; physically check! Some things to check for: ■ Audience materials ■ Activity materials ■ Toys ■ Music ■ Visual reinforcements ■ Posters ■ Videos ■ Models ■ Related books ■ Candy.	■ Trainer's kit including: 　■ Markers 　■ Scissors 　■ Masking tape 　■ Little stapler 　■ Note cards 　■ Post-it™ notes 　■ Tape flags 　■ Highlighters 　■ Pen 　■ Tape ■ Tent cards ■ Name tags ■ Construction paper ■ Stick pins.

Many trainers rely on their memory for materials, and then on the day of performance, they realize they have forgotten something and are forced to scramble to find it. Training goes much smoother when a checklist of materials is made ahead of time and materials are collected prior to the day of training.

Secure Audio/Visual Equipment

Take the time to review your A/V needs. Use your completed script to compare what you need to what you ordered. You may be surprised to find you have added some creative exercises that require additional A/V equipment. Do this far enough in advance so you can secure the additional equipment.

Flip Chart Preparation

Plan to pre-draw any flip charts you will be using in your training performance. Do not wait until the morning of the performance to draw your flip charts. You will be rushed and distracted. The results will be nonprofessional and incomplete content.

Rehearse Your Lines

Regardless of your experience or how many times you have delivered a particular performance, it is critical to rehearse. This helps bring the focus of the content back to the forefront of the actor's mind. It also helps to remind the actor of the critical parts in the performance. Rehearsing also helps actors who get nervous before a session build confidence. Rehearsing your lines includes:

- **Review the overall content**—Read your materials all the way through. Pay attention to how the material flows. Review the key points first, then the subpoints.

- **Learn your "lines"**—Learn the lines to your script so you can make regular eye contact with your audience. Many actors "read" their script and never look up at the audience. Making *eye* contact helps your audience stay connected with you and the content.

- **Rehearse with your A/V equipment**—Whenever possible, you should rehearse with your A/V equipment. This is especially important when using multiple pieces of equipment or equipment you have not used before. Whenever possible, rehearse in the room where you will be performing.

- **When using off the shelf training, rehearsal is crucial**—Rehearsing is the only way to familiarize yourself with the materials. It's imperative to practice ahead of time rather than practice on your audience.

> FYI...
> Off the shelf materials may not fit culturally with your company and may not be appropriate. Rehearsing with off the shelf products will uncover anything that could be potentially embarrassing or offensive.

MANAGE THE ENVIRONMENT

A critical part of your success relies on how aware you are or how well you manage your whole environment. Think back to a theatrical performance you have seen. How did the actors use the space? How did they react to audience reaction? Successful actors understand even with the very best writing, planning, and rehearsal, you can't always predict what will happen during the performance. You need to be ready for anything. You can also be more pro-active by constantly scanning your audience, asking yourself these questions:

- Are there audience members who are displaying negative nonverbal communication?

- Are there audience members who are displaying positive nonverbal communication?

- Is your audience getting restless?

- Is your audience showing a loss or lack of energy?

If the nonverbal cues are negative, this may be a sign that your audience needs a break, or perhaps you are going too fast and need to slow down. It may be time for an energizer. Picking up on these nonverbal cues and reacting to them can go a long way toward keeping your audience interested and learning.

Use Your Space

Don't hide or stick to one spot. Use your space effectively. Move around the room. Get out from behind the table, podium, or other things that are barriers between you and your audience. Often when presenting information for the first time, actors can be nervous. The best way to get past this is to get closer to your audience. The closer you are to your audience, the easier it is to connect with them.

Experiential Levels

Your audience's experience levels may vary in the same class. You may have people just learning the content for the first time sitting alongside others who may have a good deal of experience with the content. You will also have people who learn more quickly than others. It's important to recognize this early on and manage it. The challenge is to keep all learners engaged and learning.

> **FYI...**
>
> **A major challenge in managing the learning environment is balancing fast track learners with new learners who may be slower. One strategy is to encourage the more experienced learners to help mentor first-time learners.**

The "Parking Lot"

Occasionally, topics or questions will come up that are not related to the topic. You may not want to derail your current discussion but don't want to lose these ideas. Create a "Parking Lot" for them. To do this:

1. Place a flip chart up in front of the stage.

2. At the top of the page write the words "Parking Lot."

3. As these "off-topic" ideas are brought up throughout the training performance, "park" them by writing them on the flip chart.

4. Later in the performance, or at the end of the performance, return to the parking lot for discussion.

5. Be sure to revisit every topic in the parking lot before the training performance is over. This will ensure that all audience members achieve closure.

PERFORMANCE DAY

The planning is done and the preparations have been made. You have gone through your dress rehearsal and it is now the morning of the training performance. It is the day of the performance, and before you get on stage, you must prepare. Preparations for the day include:

- **Arrive Early**
  Always arrive early for your performance, preferably at least 60 minutes ahead of schedule. Arriving with your audience, or worse, arriving late, shows a lack of professionalism on your part. Once you have arrived, use your checklist to begin preparations.

  - Set up the room – including your props, training materials, audience materials, and handouts. Be sure everything is in the right place.

  - Walk the room – Get a general "feel" for the room and the layout of the room. This will help any last minute jitters or nervousness you may have.

- **Check the F&B for the Day**
  There is nothing worse than having a mix-up with F&B for breaks and lunch. Double-check the menus to ensure you are getting what you ordered when you want it.

- **Check All the Equipment**
  How many times have you been in a training class when the equipment breaks down and the trainer says, "Well, it worked yesterday"?

  - Check to make sure all equipment is working properly. Check lights, switches, **cue videotapes**, check connections, cables, and power.

  - Get the names of the on-site team members who can assist you with A/V and physical plant needs.

TRAINER TERMS

Cue videotapes–
fast forward or rewind videos to the place where you want them to begin. This will save time and increase your efficiency.

Performance Day Checklist

Use this checklist to make sure you have everything ready for your performance:

_____Set up the room:

    _____Training materials

    _____Audience participant handouts

    _____Toys, snacks, etc.

_____Set up Audio/Visual:

    _____Set up any PowerPoint® presentations

    _____Prepare your flip charts

    _____Cue any videotapes

    _____Check for light switches, etc.

_____Check the food & beverage for the day:

    _____Review menus

    _____Check times breaks are scheduled

    _____Confirm the number of people they are serving

_____Get names:

    _____A/V technician contact

    _____Physical plant contact (heating, cooling, lighting, etc.)

    _____Catering contact

A frequently overlooked detail occurs when trainers are using clips or sections of a video. They forget to cue the tape to the place they want it to start and then are forced to find their place in front of the audience. Not only does this look unprofessional, it causes the video to lose its impact.

CO-PERFORMING

Before closing this chapter on preparation, there is one last topic to discuss. There may be an occasion where you are co-facilitating or co-presenting with another actor. Understand that there is a difference between the two. Performing with another person is an art that requires coordination, clear transitions and practice.

Co-facilitating and **co-presenting** are different from just sharing a block of training time. Coordinating training is not the same as co-facilitating or co-presenting. While the actual techniques for facilitating or presenting are different, the mutual efforts and joint delivery are the same. Well-done co-performing takes the audience through the content and assists them in learning where, when, why, and how to apply the training. Don't be afraid to try co-performing; it can be a great experience for all.

TRAINER TERMS

Co facilitating
when both performers work together to make the training process easier by interacting simultaneously within the training experience

Co-presenting –
where each trainer introduces, offers expertise and/or consideration on the training content jointly

SKILL BUILDERS

1.   Create a pre-performance checklist of supplies, props, and materials.

2.   Take an existing mini-lecture. Key word and pre-write flip chart materials.

3.   Take an existing training and go through a complete A/V test and check.

Chapter 10

THE PERFORMANCE

Good teaching is one-fourth preparation and three-fourths theater.
— Gail Godwin

IN THIS CHAPTER:

- **Performance—Live and on Stage**
- **The Occasional Distraction**
- **Conflicts During Performance**
- **Multiple-Day Performances**
- **References**
- **Skill Builders**

Performance–Live and On Stage

All the planning, preparation, and rehearsals have led you, the actor, up to this point; bringing the story to life, live and on stage. This is the time to create an effective learning experience for the audience.

Greet the Audience

Be prepared to greet the audience as they arrive. Shake hands and introduce yourself. This will help to set the tone for the rest of the day and help your audience feel at ease. Greeting your audience can also help you learn before the performance begins.

Handling the Jitters

Every performer, regardless of how good or how experienced, faces stage fright at some point in his or her career. In fact, the fear of public speaking is one of the greatest fears in people. In his article, "Tips From the Acting World," Art Feinglass[1] offers some techniques to help overcome the jitters that accompany stage fright. These tips were borrowed from the theater:

- **Relax**—"Actors say that knowing how to relax is the most important part of their art. As much as 75% of accomplishing the desired results on stage (and in life) depend on relaxing before and during a performance. An actor's natural enemy is tension."

- **Limber up**—Practice muscle-relaxing exercises.
  - **Yawning**—This exercises the diaphragm (tension in the diaphragm can cause shortness of breath).
  - **"Tense and Release"**—An exercise where you start by slowly tightening the muscles in your toes, then feet, then legs, and so on until every muscle in your body is tense. Then relax all the muscles at once. Repeat several times.

- **Take deep breaths**—Typically, when you are nervous or scared, the instinct is to take shallow, quick breaths. This only adds to the jitters.

- **Be prepared**—The best way to get rid of nervous tension is to know your lines.

- **Eat right and get plenty of rest.**
    - **Eat breakfast**—Your body will need the fuel to make it through the day. Try to keep it healthy! A donut and coffee is not the type breakfast we are talking about here! Have fruit, eggs, or yogurt.
    - **Drink only a small amount of caffeine**—Many people think caffeine is the fuel to get going in the morning. The reality is too much caffeine will make you jittery.
    - **Get a good night sleep**—The best thing you can do to calm your nerves is to be well rested. You will think and act better.
- **Visualize a calm place**—Close your eyes. Draw a mental picture of a place that represents tranquility to you. Visualize yourself in that place.
- **Visualize success**—Think back to a time when you did something very successfully. Remember how that felt. Think about the things you did to make it successful. This will help boost your self-confidence.
- **Lose yourself in the script**—Rehearse so you feel you know the information. Focus on the content and delivering it to the audience.

Ask the Audience Questions

Asking questions is a great way to encourage audience participation. Today's audience wants to take an active part in their learning. You can get them involved by asking for their personal experiences. Some basics to keep in mind when asking questions:

- Keep questions clear and simple
- Emphasize one idea or point
- Use open-ended questions
- Require a specific answer.

Handling Incorrect Answers

Undoubtedly the audience will answer some of your questions incorrectly. How you handle wrong answers will enhance or hinder the learning experience. The one thing you don't want to do is to publicly humiliate the person who gave you the wrong answer. It will not only embarrass that person; it will stop others from even trying. Worse yet, it will interfere with future learning. When incorrect answers are given, respond by saying, "That's an interesting perspective," or "That's a good answer, but I am looking for something a little different." Be aware when you are giving feedback of how you say things—do not give inaccurate feedback, which could lead the learner to think he or she was correct.

The Occasional Distraction

It is not uncommon for a participant's attention to "check in and out" at various times during the performance. In other words, each participant is only listening part of the time. Their minds wander, regardless of whether they are distracted, disconnected, or just plain bored.

Two people attending the same performance can come out with two completely different perspectives. What one person takes away from a particular interaction can differ completely from what another takes away. The reason is each has checked in and out at different times during the performance, resulting in hearing different things.

In and Out Thinking

You should first understand what "In and Out" thinking is. Humans can hear and comprehend approximately 900-950 words per minute. Most of us are able to speak only about 150 words per minute. Since our minds think faster than people speak, a person is fully attentive only during the first 13-18 seconds of a communication. Then they begin to fade "Out." Their mind will wander for a period of time and then fade back "In." They will pay attention for another 13-18 seconds and the pattern will repeat itself.[2]

The question is how do we make sure the learner is taking away the key points of the performance while this is occurring? One way is to utilize a method of note taking known as "In and Out" note taking. This method provides audiences with an organized way of not only capturing key elements from the performance, but also allows them to capture random thoughts running through their minds during the performance. You need to teach the audience how to use this method of note taking.

■ Instruct audience members to take a sheet of paper and draw a vertical line down the middle of the paper, creating two columns.

■ At the top of the left column, write the word "IN."

■ At the top of the right column, write the word "OUT."

- Ask the audience to use the left column to take notes on key points of the performance during the time when they are checking "in" to the learning.

- Ask the audience to use the right column to write down any notes or issues they think about when their minds begin to wander or when they are checked "out" of the performance.

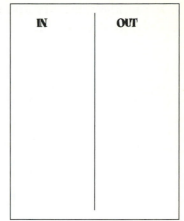

IN	OUT

"In and Out"
Note Taking Method

This may seem odd at first and certainly out of the norm of what we are taught in school. The magic of this type of note taking, however, is it allows people to jot down notes in the "Out" column about things that are prompted by the content you are discussing. Allowing them to capture what they are thinking at the time frees them to check back "in" to the performance sooner!

Be Flexible

Today's learning environment forces you to be flexible. Being too rigid can cause you to fail. Accept the fact that things will happen during your performance which you are not anticipating. Adjust as needed and allow yourself to go with the flow.

Conflicts During the Performance

Every performer has encountered uncomfortable situations during a performance. It could be a talkative group in the back of the room, ringing cell phones or pagers, or an over-aggressive audience member. What is the proper way to handle these situations? Start by limiting the possibility of them ever happening. Set the standard prior to your performance. Request cell phones and pagers be turned off or switched to the silent function. Ask all comments or questions be preceded by the old standard of raising your hand. Here are some thoughts on handling conflicts:

- Handling conflicts starts at the beginning of the performance by discussing class norms and expectations. By doing this, if someone becomes disruptive you can redirect their energy by reminding them of the earlier discussion.

- Handle conflicts immediately and calmly. Aggressive behavior invites aggressive behavior.

- Take control of the situation by inviting the person to "reconsider their actions." Be fair, firm, and consistent. Never embarrass the person by arguing or challenging him or her in front of the audience. Note: Ignoring the behavior will cause you to lose control.

- If the disruptive audience member continues his or her misbehavior, invite him or her to leave the learning environment.

- In more serious situations, you may call for a break and take the person out into a hall or other room and talk to him or her in private. Again try to keep the situation calm.

- Try to resolve the situation so that everyone wins.

Should you still encounter disruptions during your performance, you must handle them immediately. Take control of every situation letting the attendees know who is in charge. If you allow the audience to control the learning atmosphere, you will lose your credibility.

Troubleshooting the Classroom

The majority of all problems that occur during a performance involve one of two areas: the physical plant or your equipment.

Physical Plant

Issue	Solution
Room Temperature	■ Prior to the performance, have the temperature set 5 degrees below comfortable. Expect the room to heat up during your performance. ■ Make adjustments during breaks.
Loss of Lighting	■ Contact maintenance and request repair or replacement during your break.
Power Outage	■ Know the facility's procedures prior to performance. ■ Know the exit plan for the facility.
Restroom Issues	■ Contact maintenance and request immediate repair.

Equipment

As you know from the "dress rehearsal," you should already be prepared with a low-tech backup for any issues you may have with high-tech equipment. Remember to run pre-checks on your equipment prior to your performance. If you do run into an issue with a piece of A/V equipment, remain calm and use your backup plan. If appropriate, consider adjusting your break time.

MULTIPLE-DAY PERFORMANCES

There are several things you need to consider when conducting a multiple-day seminar. The opening for your first day should include greeting the audience as they arrive, overviewing the schedule for the day, and sharing your classroom "rules." For subsequent training, days open with the following:

- **Recap and Review**—A great way to start the day is with a review of the day before. There are several ways to do this. Some good ways are to:
  - Assign topics to audience members at the close of the performance the night before and have them report on them the next morning.
  - Play a game using concepts from the day before.
  - Use flip charts to write key concepts on each page and hang them around the room. Assign the pages to small groups and have them do brief reviews for the entire audience.
- **Icebreaker or Energizer**—Start each day with an activity to get the audience's energy level up and refocused on the class. The more audience participation, the better.
- **The Agenda**—Review the agenda for the day. You don't need to go through the housekeeping notes, but you may want to remind everyone about the norms before getting started.

Stop, Start, Continue

While you will be doing a formal evaluation on the last day of the seminar, it's a good idea to "check in" with your audience on a daily basis. One quick way to do this is with a "Stop, Start, and Continue" activity. The idea is to allow your audience to give quick anonymous feedback on how they think the training is going.

Consider the following:

- On a flip chart, draw two vertical lines, dividing the flip chart into thirds or have three flip charts lined up.
- On the top of one column or one flip chart, write the words "Start Doing."
- On top of the middle column or flip chart, write the words "Stop Doing."
- On top of the third column or flip chart, write the words "Continue Doing."
- Supply Post-it™ notes to each table.
- Ask your audience to write something they want you to stop doing on one Post-it™ note, something they want you to continue doing on another, and something they want you to start doing on a third Post-it™ note.
- If they don't have anything to write, that's OK. The goal is to provide those audience members who have feedback a way of giving it to you.
- Place the flip chart(s) near the door.
- Ask your audience to place their Post-it™ notes under their respective headings as they exit the room for the day.
- Take the time to read the Post-it™ notes. Continue to do the things they liked and consider the things they didn't like.
- As a part of your opening the next morning, review their feedback. Let your audience know what your plans are. If there are things that are beyond your control and can't change, make sure you explain why you couldn't change it.

You can also ask your audience to write any comments they have on a blank flip chart, giving you any feedback they have or anything they would like to talk about that wasn't covered in the day's session.

Daily Closings

When closing the last day of a multiple-day seminar, use the "Closing" recommended in Writing Your Script (page 110). For each of the other days, there are several things you can do.

Say Thank You—Thank your audience for all their hard work. Recognize any outstanding contributions made by any audience members that day.

Set Up Tomorrow—Let your audience know what to expect for tomorrow. Remind them what time the session starts and ends.

A Quick Review—Summarize the key concepts of the day and how they relate to the remaining concepts of the training performance.

At the close of a session, ask audience members to write one question they think everyone in the class should be prepared to answer which is specific to the training they just received. Collect the questions and read them aloud for an instant review. Note: This technique can also be used throughout the session as well as to collect a base for future written evaluations.

REFERENCES

1. Feinglass, Art. "Tips From the Acting World." Training and Development, August, 2000. Pages 20-21.

2. Firestien, Roger L., Foucar-szocki, Diane. *Breakthrough to Ideas*. Multiple Resource Media. 1983.

SKILL BUILDERS

1. Write a personal plan for handling jitters.

2. Set up your own methods for taking personal notes on your performance. Identify how you will utilize planned evaluations to help you refine ongoing performances.

3. Categorize each activity on a multiple-day training. Audit each activity for variety and audience interaction.

Chapter 11

THE REVIEWS

A teacher is one who makes himself progressively unnecessary.
— Thomas Carruthers

IN THIS CHAPTER:

- **So... How Well Are You Doing?**
- **Performance-Based Perspective**
- **Return on Investment**
- **Calculating ROI**
- **Skill Builders**

So...How Well Are You Doing?

Measurement and evaluation are considered to be interchangeable terms. Both require a review of:

- Your materials
- The performance
- The learning taking place.

There are several critiques, or measurements, your training must pass: Did the audience learn what they were supposed to? Did you contribute to the business goals of the organization? Is the audience able to transfer what they have learned to the workplace?

As a company looks to improve the performance of its employees, it follows that they would want to improve continuously the quality of training. Companies must measure current training results. Actors/trainers tend to view evaluations of their abilities to perform as a necessary evil. Try viewing evaluations as a way of realizing opportunities to refine your training.

Measuring Training

The concept of measurement is not new. The primary source for measurement over the last four decades has been Kirkpatrick's Four Levels of Evaluation model – introduced in 1959. These four levels of evaluation include:

Level One: Reaction

Measures reaction to training and customer satisfaction.

- Measurement tools include **smile sheets** and reaction sheets.

TRAINER TERMS

Smile Sheets -
A term used to refer to a reaction sheet or a "mini-survey" which is designed to survey the audience on a training performance

Level Two: Learning

Measures learning: What knowledge was learned? What skills were developed or improved? What attitudes were changed?

- Measurement tools include pre-/post-assessments and paper and pencil tests.

Level Three: Behavior

Measures how much of the knowledge, skills, and attitudes learned during training have transferred back to the job.

- Measurement tools include pre-/post-assessments, surveys, and interviews of employees' supervisors.

Level Four: Results

Measures the results or the impact on the organization due to the training.

- Measurement tools include pre-/post-assessments and cost vs. benefit analysis.[1]

Kirkpatrick's 4 Levels	Definition	Measurement Tools
Level One: Reaction	Measures reaction to training; measures customer satisfaction	■ Smile sheets ■ Reaction sheets
Level Two: Learning	Measures learning or what knowledge was learned	■ Pre-/post-assessments ■ Paper & pencil tests
Level Three: Behavior	Measures how much of the knowledge, skills, and attitudes have changed the on-the-job results	■ Pre-/post-surveys ■ Interviews with supervisors
Level Four: Results	Measures the impact on the organization based on the training	■ Pre-/post-assessments ■ Cost vs. benefits analysis

While Kirkpatrick's model has been around for decades, most training today is still measured only to the extent of Level One. Why is this the case? "The simplest thing to evaluate about a training program is the trainees' immediate reaction to it... The hardest thing to measure is the concrete benefit a given training initiative actually brings to the business that pays for the training."[2]

Measurement Today

The 21st century approach to learning and measurement, with its roots in Kirkpatrick's model, has evolved to a performance-based perspective. Brook Manville, in his article, "Learning in the Future," states, "Varieties of learning that don't translate into customer satisfaction and profitability, growth or employee retention will fall away. Measures that tell you about the health of your business will be what matters – and smart companies will make those measurements early in the learning process."[3]

More simply stated, the goal is to measure how effectively training is contributing to the success of the business and its employees. This 21st century paradigm focuses on organizational needs, economic potential, and the needs of the stakeholder.[4]

PERFORMANCE-BASED PERSPECTIVE

It's no longer enough just to provide training to an audience. Training must be focused on the standards of performance, driving business results, and achieving business goals. Additionally, it's not enough just to measure whether a training performance was good or not. It's not even enough to measure whether an employee skill level or behavior change is a result of the training. While these things are important and should certainly be considered, the ultimate measurement is:

- **How well the employee consistently performs against the standard in the workplace**.

To effectively operate within this new paradigm of performance-based instruction, measurement can no longer occur exclusively at the end of a training session. It is necessary to thread measurement throughout the entire learning experience. Measurement tools need to be identified from the design of the training to on-the-job performance and beyond.

Cycle of Performance-Based Training

A model that can provide a systematic approach to how we look at training and measurement from this new paradigm is The Cycle of Performance-Based

Training. This emerging model takes a holistic approach to training and measurement by threading the levels of measurement through the entire training experience. The cycle of performance-based training includes:

- Measurement of audience knowledge throughout the training experience
- Behavioral measurement of how employees transfer what they learned into the workplace
- Measurement of business results
- Measurement of the quality of training from the audience's perspective
- Performance-based training is grounded in the belief successful training begins with linking the training directly to the business strategy and goals. Training is ultimately deemed successful when business results are improved and operational goals have been achieved.

The Cycle of Performance-Based Training

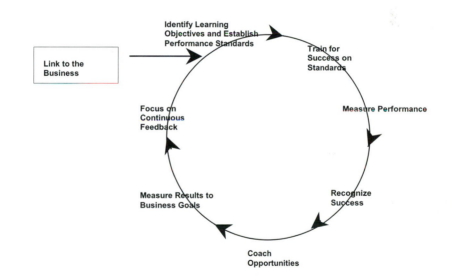

Link to the Business Strategy and Goals

Today's savvy actor/trainer knows training must be linked directly to business strategy and goals. When designing your measurement of training, you must consider the company's mission, vision, goals, and key initiatives. The operational business partners, like department managers, are essential to your training success.

Identify the Learning Objectives and Set the Performance Standards

Once measurable learning objectives have been set, you need to establish clear standards of performance for each objective. As you will recall, standards of performance are the clear expectations of the worker for the task or job. When setting performance standards, be sure to consider the following:

- Identify specific standards or best practices associated with the objectives
- Break down the steps to the task or job
- Establish a measurement for each step
- Review specific job **competencies**.

The more details, the easier it will be to measure success.

Competencies

Patricia McLagan, in her article "Competencies: The Next Generation," defines competencies in the following way:

Task Competencies: These are usually defined as job tasks or activities. The tasks are the "result of many years of breaking work down into manageable activities and procedures in order to lessen the amount of thinking needed to eliminate performance variability, and to spread best practices."

Result Competencies: Result competencies define a result. An example would be "the ability to produce profits." These are less common than task competencies.

Knowledge, Skills, and Attitude Competencies: "In this case, subject matter (such as engineering knowledge); process abilities (such as listening skills); and attitudes, values, orientations, and commitments (such as integrity and achievement) are called competencies..."[5]

Train for Success on the Standards

Once the learning objectives and standards of performance have been set, you must determine how to train to meet these standards. As we have discussed in previous chapters, an effective training performance not only includes the topic, it requires consideration of who the audience is and what their knowledge and skill levels are. It also calls for you to consider what type of delivery is required, add creativity, write an effective script, incorporate experiential learning activities, use technology when appropriate, and thread measurement throughout the experience.

Brief supervisors and managers on what their employees will be learning. Give them a quick review of the specific skills they can look for in their employees when they return to the job. The clearer your information, the likelier you are to get the assistance of the supervisor in helping the transfer of learning.

Measuring Performance Against the Standard

Once the training performance is complete, you need to measure the audience's knowledge of the content and their effectiveness in transferring the learning to the job. This process should measure the audience's performance on the job against the standards and behaviors they were trained on. Use preplanned measurement tools to assess their performance in the workplace. Share your measurement tools with the audience before they are used and when you are reviewing your results. Effective measurement tools can include:

- Script audits
- Telephone audits
- Observation checklists

FYI...

"When done well, assessment becomes indistinguishable from the learning process itself. People integrate information through their own thought processes – not simply by receiving information."[6]

- Inspections
- Quality audits
- Secret shoppers
- Skill-based certification tests.

If you are relying on supervisors and managers to conduct the measurement, be sure to provide them with the measurement tools you want them to use. You may need to train the supervisors on the proper utilization of the measurement tools.

Note: The following listing of key measurements is meant to provide examples and is not necessarily inclusive of all key measurements.

Script Audits

A simple form which lists 10-15 behaviors that should be displayed in interactions with customers, with points allocated to each item.

Uses: Measures the use of prescribed words and actions in an interaction with a customer.

Example: A 10-point script audit measuring how well a hostess greets people at the door of a restaurant.

Advantages: Easy to use as a quick tool to measure usage of taught skills.

Telephone Audits

Same as script audit but designed for telephone interaction.

Uses: Measures the use of prescribed words and actions in an interaction with customers over the phone.

Example: A 15-point telephone audit measuring how well a catalogue operator speaks with the customer.

Advantages: Easy to use as a quick tool to measure usage of taught skills.

Observation Checklists

A checklist, listing required behaviors for a particular position or job, with points allocated to each item.

Uses: Measures performance for any job or position requiring demonstrable behaviors.

Example: A 20-point checklist listing the steps for assembling a widget. Measures ability to demonstrate each of the steps.

Advantage: Helps quantify demonstrable skills.

Disadvantages: Depending on the job, it could be time-consuming.

Inspections

A process or checklist outlining required outcomes or results for a given job.

Uses: Measures quality of work for any job or position.

Example: A 20-point inspection checklist measuring the cleanliness of a guest room after a housekeeper has cleaned it.

Advantages: Effective for measuring results if you share the outcomes with the people responsible for the work.

Disadvantages: Time-consuming and could miss things.

Quality Audits

A process or checklist outlining required outcomes or results for a given job.

Uses: Measures compliance on required behaviors.

Example: A 30-point safety audit, measuring compliance on all safety issues for the company.

Advantages: Sets very clear expectations.

Disadvantages: Can be intimidating for those being audited.

Secret Shoppers

A process where a customer or employee posing as a customer uses a checklist and enters a business undercover and conducts the audit.

Uses: Measures compliance or performance for specific required behaviors.

Example: A 20-point checklist used to measure the way a customer service employee handles customer complaints.

Advantages: Very effective for unannounced audits and to observe employees in real-life settings.

Disadvantages: There can be inconsistency, due to the variety and number of "secret shoppers."

Certification Tests

Testing which may include a written component, a demonstrable component, and an inspection component.

Uses: Measures technical knowledge and is used typically after training and some type of practice, apprenticeship, or demonstration.

Example: A 50-point written test on the knowledge of upgrading various types of computers. A 100-point demonstrable skills assessment on ability and three unannounced inspections of computers you have worked on.

Advantages: Very thorough and all-inclusive.

Disadvantages: Can be time-consuming and intimidating to the employee.

Actors and managers often want to use tools immediately after the employee gets back to the workplace. It's important to allow the employee some time to practice. Waiting several days, up to a week, provides a more accurate picture of the long-term effect of the training.

Recognize Success

You need to share your assessments with the audience member. One way to reinforce positive behavior is through recognition. The more specific you can make the recognition, the more of an impact you can have on the learner's behavior. Using your assessments as a basis for recognition is much more meaningful than simply telling an employee "great job!"

Use competitions and incentives as a way to recognize performance and improvement.

Coaching Opportunities

A critical step often missed in the measurement of training effectiveness is coaching and correcting audience members who are performing at sub-par levels. If an employee has completed the training and is not successful, it's your job as the actor to identify their challenges. Take the time to coach and teach the employee until he or she has reached the goal. Use your measurement tools to uncover specific challenges and pinpoint behaviors that need to be reinforced through additional training or coaching.

FYI...
If, in the evaluation process, you uncover several employees that are having the same challenges and opportunities, the training may be flawed.

Compare Results to Business Goals

The ultimate measure of successful training is the accomplishment of the quantifiable business goals. Setting the standards, training on the standards, and measuring employee performance against those standards are done to accomplish specific business goals. Even though this is often difficult to measure, take the time to determine whether or not the training initiative had an impact on the business. "The hardest thing to measure is the concrete benefit a given training initiative actually brings to a business."[7]

Actors often attribute all business results to the training performance. This may not always be the case. Other factors in the business environment may have contributed to the success of the goals. Showing a direct correlation between the training and business results will strengthen the argument that training had a direct impact.

Focus on Continuous Feedback

The Performance-Based Training Cycle is completed by eliciting feedback from the audience members on their perspective of the training class itself. According to Julie Tamminen, of the Motely Fool Investment Web site, "When evaluating training, businesses should apply the same common-sense values to internal customers as to external customers."[8] If that is the case, then actors should survey their "internal customers," the employees, just as companies survey their external customers. Surveying the "internal customers" can take on many forms, from smile sheets to evaluations. They can be done anytime—the day of training or after the employees return to the job.

An Example - A Business Application

Linking to the Business...

Part of the mission of the Market Bank is to become the "bank known for customer service." A key initiative of the bank is to improve the customer service skills of every employee working there. They have implemented a "Customer Service" feedback survey for their banking customers. Upper management at the bank has set a business goal: a consolidated score of 90% customer satisfaction as reported on the surveys by the end of the year. In other words, 90% of all the customers that completed the survey need to rate their customer service experience as a 9 or a 10 (on a scale of 1-10, with 10 being great customer service and 1 being poor customer service).

(continued)

An Example - A Business Application (continued)

To accomplish this goal, Tom, the Market Bank training manager, was given the challenge of training employees to meet the goal. First Tom identified the learning objectives to the goal. Based upon conversations with key stakeholders in the bank, two learning objectives emerged:

- Every employee will demonstrate customer service techniques impacting bank customers.

- Employees will shift from task orientation to a service orientation with bank customers.

Tom turned to the management team at the bank for assistance. Together, they had three months to identify how they would accomplish the specific learning objectives, set the standards of performance, train the employees, and measure results against the business goal.

Setting the Performance Standards

Together, Tom and the bank managers established standards of performance to accomplish the learning objectives. They identified three key areas to work on: Telephone etiquette, greeting zones, and service recovery (handling customer complaints).

Through a brainstorming session, they developed a set of standards and requirements as a blueprint for each area. These blueprints were the basis for developing a training performance. Each of the standards included the key skills, knowledge, and personal attributes required to drive outstanding performance. They also provided every employee with a common language around customer service. This allowed them to clearly communicate with each other and their supervisors as issues came up in the workplace.

Training for Success

Now, with the help of the bank managers, Tom set the standards and developed the training performance to train the employees. He kept the class focused and included experiential learning and "knowledge checks" along the way. Tom knew testing knowledge throughout the process was important.

Measure Performance Against the Standard

Now for the real test! Tom knew his audience understood the new standards and could perform them. The real key was determining how "sticky" the

(continued)

An Example - A Business Application (continued)

training was and how it changed behavior in the workplace. He recognized that the audience would only achieve the goal if they applied what they learned on the job!

To measure behavior, Tom used script audits and observation checklists. Tom trained the management team on how to do observation checklists and script audits. Additionally, Tom coached the managers on how to praise and reinforce good work. Finally, he showed them how to use these measurement tools as an on-the-job training aid for continuous improvement.

Recognize Success

Tom built in incentives for audience members who did a great job implementing what they had learned. Each time an employee received a score of 100% on their script audit, the recognition program rewarded them.

Coach Opportunities

Tom recognized that not everyone would be executing exactly to the standard immediately. Coaching and encouragement practices were rooted throughout the team.

Measure Business Goals

Each month the scores and measurements were reviewed. Not only did they accomplish the goal, they reached it two periods early.

Focus on Continuous Feedback

Everyone at Market Bank was extremely pleased with the results. Tom knows to continue the success; it is a good practice to review results regularly and to seek feedback from all stakeholders.

Intangible Measures

Not every training initiative should be measured to the same degree. According to Jack Phillips, "Not all measures can or should be converted to monetary values. By design, some are captured and reported as intangible measures. Although they may not be perceived as being as valuable as the measures converted to monetary values, intangible measures are critical to the overall evaluation process."[9]

When the Training is Complete

What happens after training is often more important than what happens during it. Twenty-first century training professionals understand that their job doesn't end when the training performance ends. To consistently help drive performance in the organizations:

- Work with intact work groups and hold followup meetings on issues and opportunities within the work units
- Find ways for employees who are struggling to partner with other audience members who attended the same training performance
- Reinforce content from the training performance by posting visual aids, posters, and key phrase job aids in break areas and employee areas
- Continuously solicit feedback.

RETURN ON INVESTMENT

The "bottom line" of measurement is it is here to stay. The better you become at execution, the more successful you will be. Remember, what gets measured gets done.

Just as a business measures the return on any financial investment, training professionals must measure their return on training investments. The first step is changing the attitude from "training is a cost to the company" to "training is an investment the company makes in its people and its future." The challenge is that many training professionals still believe this can't be done. The argument is: while we can accurately calculate training costs, it's very difficult to measure or quantify the results of training or the specific financial impact training has upon the organization. Many businesses are now expecting a Return on Investment (ROI) analysis from the training department, just as it does from all its other departments.

ROI Defined

ROI is the measurement that compares program costs to monetary benefits. In other words, what is the payback to the company on the money spent on training? The results of the ROI analysis are usually presented as a percent or a cost/benefit ratio.[10] Time and money are always components of this formula.

The Goal of ROI

Focus on the "right training" or training that has the greatest impact on the organization and its people and yields the greatest payback. ROI is the measurement that will allow us to focus on training that has the greatest impact on the organization.

It's important to note that not all training programs should be measured in terms of ROI. Determining ROI is very time-consuming and can be difficult to calculate. Only programs tied into high priority business issues should be considered. Calculate the ROI for programs requiring a significant investment of money or programs that impact large numbers of people in the organization.

The Challenges of ROI

One of the greatest challenges of the ROI analysis is trying to isolate the impact of a specific training performance from other influences that may be occurring at the same time as the training. Be prepared to show correlations when cause and effect is not obvious. One way to show a direct impact would be to evaluate specific behaviors that are directly attributable to the training performance. Another would be to compare the results of employees who had attended the training performance versus those who had not. Better results from those trained would show a direct correlation between the training and the results.

An Example

A new manager has just started in the shipping and receiving department of your company. The training department conducted a training performance on customer service skills shortly thereafter. Approximately half the employees in the shipping and receiving department attended the class. Within a month of training, the customer service surveys showed that customers were pleased with the service they were receiving and rated the company very high. Customer services ratings had increased 2% over the previous month.

(continued)

(continued)

The question: Was it the manager or was it the training performance that impacted the results? It was probably a bit of both. If this is the case, how can we accurately measure the impact of the training performance? An analysis of individual employee ratings yielded concrete results. What they discovered was that every employee who had attended the training performance averaged a 1-2% higher customer service rating than those employees who had not attended.

Calculating ROI

ROI can be a very complex process. Jack J. Phillips, in his book *Return on Investment,* goes into significant detail on the ROI process as it relates to training. There are five major steps to calculating ROI:

1. List all the costs of training (including development, delivering the performance, wages, trainer salaries, etc.)

2. Determine the savings or benefits of the program (including increased quantity, less defects, lower accidents, etc.)

3. Do the math:

   ((Savings - costs)/costs) X 100 = ROI

4. Compare the ROI for the training program to the standard ROI your company will accept as a minimum return on any investment they make.

5. You and your stakeholders then need to determine if the training program is worth the investment.

The Costs

The first step in the ROI analysis is to determine costs. There are several costs to consider. Most costs are quantifiable and relatively obvious. The more obvious ones include (but are not limited to):

■ Cost of development of the program
■ Cost of supplies for the development
■ Trainer salary

- Cost of delivering training performance including:
    - Supplies
    - Cost of meeting room
    - Cost of travel (for attendees and trainer)
    - Cost of F&B (food and beverage)
    - Cost of administering the training.

There are other costs that are less obvious and sometimes forgotten. To get an accurate ROI, these must be included in the calculation as well. They include:

- Cost of attendee salary or wages
- Loss of productivity/time away from job while attending training
- Cost of replacement personnel on job while attendees are in training
- Special requirements for the training.

The Savings

Now that we have a clear picture of the costs, the second step is to determine the savings of the program. Again, part of the challenge is being able to show the direct correlation between the training and the benefits. It is also challenging to put a dollar amount to some of the outcomes of training. Some potential benefits include:

> **FYI...**
>
> Many trainers still measure the training function by activities rather than results. As Amy Purcell writes in her article: "20/20 ROI," "Many trainers don't take evaluation to Kirkpatrick's Level 4 results; even fewer take it to Jack J. Phillips' Level 5, ROI – the monetary value of training results exceeding the cost of training."[11]

> **TRAINER TERMS**
>
> **Costs** -
>   all costs associated with the development and delivery of the training performance
>
> **Savings** -
>   all savings, due to performance improvement, occurring because of the delivery of the program and the transfer of learning back to the work environment
>
> **Net Program Benefits** -
>   all savings less all costs associated with the development and delivery of the program

- More quantity – amount of money gained through more quantity (labor saving for increased production)
- Less defects – amount of money saved through fewer defects
- Less accidents – amount of money saved through lower accident costs
- Less tardy/absenteeism – amount of money saved through gained productivity
- Higher productivity – amount of money saved through increase in productivity

- Time savings – amount saved through efficiencies in time (assign an average hourly wage to the reduced time requiring scheduling)

- Reduction in turnover – amount saved through increased productivity and additional training costs

- Higher customer satisfaction – amount saved through repeat customers.

The more we can show a direct correlation between a specific training performance and business results, the stronger the ROI argument is. It's not enough to say we did some training and it reduced turnover. While we know training does have an impact on turnover, we have to be able to show the direct connection and calculate the ROI. A dollar value needs to be assigned to this discussion.

Net Program Benefits

Net program benefits are the program savings minus program costs.[12] In other words, once you have calculated your costs and your savings, subtract costs from savings. This will give you your net program benefits.

The Calculation

Once you have all your information, it's time to do the math! First subtract program costs from program savings. Then divide net program benefits by the program costs. Multiply the answer by 100 to put the results into a percentage.[13]

The percentage you get is the return on investment for the training initiative.

Net Program Benefits = Program Savings - Program Costs

$$ROI = \frac{\text{Net Program Benefits}}{\text{Program Cost}} \times 100$$

The company expects to make, or save, a specific amount of money as a direct result of the training. Company policy may dictate an acceptable threshold for a successful ROI. Many companies use 25% as the minimum return they will accept on an investment.

An Example - ROI Calculation

You have developed a training performance on life safety issues. It is being developed for every employee in the company. You will hold 10 training performances at different times to allow everyone to attend.

The Costs:

Development Costs	**$25,000**
Facilitation Costs (10 performances for the year)	**$ 4,000**
Handbook scripts for audience members (10 classes, 20 audience members per performance, $20 per audience script to copy, collate, and bind)	**$ 4,000**
Meals/Meeting Room/Facility Costs ($50 per day per person)	**$10,000**
Actors' Salary & Benefits	**$ 6,650**
Audience Members' Salary & Benefits	**$21,280**
Total Cost	**$70,930**

The Savings:

Reduction of on-the-job accidents (lower medical costs, lost time)	**$100,000**
Reduction in number of defects	**$ 30,000**
Total Savings	**$130,000**

The Formula:

The Savings - The Costs = Net Program Savings

$130,000 - $70,930 = $59,070

$$ROI = \frac{\text{Net Program Savings}}{\text{Program Costs}} \times 100$$

$$ROI = \frac{59,070}{70,930} \times 100$$

ROI = 83%

The company threshold for deciding whether to invest or not is a 25% return on investment. In this example, the training was well worth the investment!

REFERENCES

1. Kirkpatrick, Donald. L. *Evaluating Training Programs: The Four Levels*. Berrett-Koehler Publishers, Inc. San Francisco. 1996.

2. Bergman, Peter and Howie Jacobson. "Yes, You Can Measure the Business Results of Training." Training. August 2000 pages 68-72.

3. Manville, Brook. "Learning in the Future." Fast Company. October 2000. p. 114.

4. Schroeder, Daniel. "Measuring Up." Biztimes.com. April 2000. pp. 15-16.

5. McLagan, Patrica A. "Competencies: The Next Generation." Training & Development. May 1997. pp. 40-47.

6. Sister Joel Read. "If You Get an A." Fast Company. October 2000 p. 106.

7. Bergman, Peter and Howie Jacobson. "Yes, You Can Measure the Business Results of Training." Training. August 2000 pp. 68-72.

8. Abernathy, Donna. "Thinking Outside the Evaluation Box." Training & Development. February 1999 pp. 19-23.

9. Phillips, Jack. As cited in Abernathy, Donna. "Thinking Outside the Evaluation Box" Training & Development. February 1999 pp. 19-23.

10. Phillips, Jack J. *Return on Investment*. Gulf Publishing Company. Houston. 1997.

11. Amy Purcell. "20/20 ROI." Training & Development. July 2000 pp. 28-31.

12. Phillips, Jack J. *Return on Investment*. Gulf Publishing Company. Houston. 1997.

13. Phillips, Jack J. *Return on Investment*. Gulf Publishing Company. Houston. 1997.

SKILL BUILDERS

1. Design a smile sheet (mini-survey) for a mini-lecture.

2. Review standards of performance supporting training you have designed. Identify the knowledge, skills, and attitudes required for successful performance. Map each standard of performance against the measurable goals and objectives.

3. Create a supervisor's observation sheet to audit measurable knowledge, skills, and attitudes that were the focus of the training.

4. Calculate the return on investment (ROI) for a specific training. Use the described formula in this book.

Chapter 12

E-LEARNING BASICS

Technology is a great productivity enhancer, but it cannot change the fundamentals of human communication. — Ron Zemke

IN THIS CHAPTER:

- **Training with Technology**
- **What Is E-Learning?**
- **Is E-learning for You?**
- **Designing E-learning**
- **The Future of E-learning**
- **Tech Terms**
- **References**
- **Skill Builders**

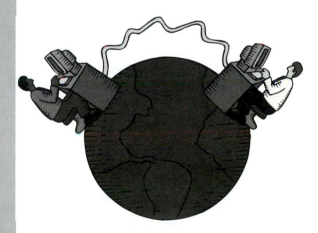

TRAINING WITH TECHNOLOGY

One of the newest trends in training is to incorporate technology into the performance. The computer is now becoming a viable tool for providing training. Advances in technology are making it possible to deliver training over long distances and to bring together diverse groups of people from across the country for relatively little cost. Technology is giving us new ways to deliver material, from interactive group sessions and computer simulations, to on-demand training sessions, customized for each learner.

At the heart of this new shift is constantly improving technology and a work force with limited attention spans who are consistently being required to process more information in a shorter time. The way in which people learn, the speed at which we are required to learn, and when we learn have all changed.

Distance-learning is learning that takes places in one location while the instructor is in another. Forms of distance-learning include on-line learning, correspondence classes, and courses by television or cable.

- **On-line Learning** is educational materials presented on a computer that links to learning resources outside the course.
- **CBT or Computer-Based Training** includes courses presented on a computer that are usually not linked to learning resources outside the course.
- **E-learning (Electronic Learning)** is material presented electronically to the learner on a computer via the Internet, corporate intranet, or CD-ROM.

This chapter will focus on the elements of E-learning.

WHAT IS E-LEARNING?

Using the computer to deliver training is the most popular mode of electronic learning. An E-learning program generally includes:

- Delivery on a computer via the Internet, intranet, or CD-ROM
- Video, graphic, audio, and text elements to engage the learner
- Short, interactive training modules, 5-10 minutes long
- Modules that can be customized to the needs of the individual learner

- Access to additional materials on the Internet or corporate intranet
- Individualized performance tracking through testing and record keeping.

Benefits of E-learning

Why has E-learning created so much interest and excitement? The possibilities are endless and the benefits can be great. E-learning provides:

- **Just-in-time learning** that helps people learn at their own pace, and when it is convenient for them
- **Interactive and flexible** delivery of information
- **Training customized** to the individual needs of each learner
- **Cost effective** ways to deliver information (in some cases eliminating the needs for classroom, trainer, and expenses of training classes)
- **Centralized performance tracking** that allows reports to be generated that show performance of individuals, groups, and regions
- **Expandable training** that allows additional modules to be added as needed
- **Follow up opportunities for classroom training** that provides extra practice and the opportunity to reinforce lessons learned in traditional training settings.

TRAINER TERMS

CD-ROM -
disk used to store text, audio, video, graphics, etc.
Internet -
An interconnected system of networks that connects computers around the world
Intranet -
a network that is only available to people who work within the company

FYI . . .
"The benefit for companies implementing E-learning programs is that they can do more training, in less time, for more people, in more locations, with fewer resources."[1]
- Robert Koolen

Challenges of E-learning

E-learning is still in the early stages of development. As with any new technology, there are always challenges to its use.

- **Poorly designed materials**—Many people convert textbook materials to an electronic book and consider that E-learning. Designing E-learning materials involves a different set of rules than classroom training does.

- **Lack of adequate equipment**—Computer system requirements, networking, and connectivity issues.

- **Cost**—Developing good E-learning programs can be expensive including large internal development costs or outsourcing costs. Periodic updating of materials can be expensive.

- **Works best for certain types of learning**—
Not all training is effective in an E-learning format. Developing personal connections and relationships can be difficult in E-learning.

- **Perceptions of management and learners**—
Many people still don't understand it. They are skeptical of learning that is not in a classroom.

- **Lack of computer skills**—There is still a large population that has not learned to use a computer or that have limited computer skills.

> FYI . . .
> Fifty percent of the U.S. work force still doesn't know how to use a computer.[2]

- **Development time**—It can be time-consuming to design and create effective E-learning. Materials need to be updated periodically to remain current.

IS E-LEARNING FOR YOU?

E-learning can be very costly to implement. Before deciding this is the direction in which your company should go, there are some things you should consider:

- **Do a company-wide technology capability audit**—Many companies may not have the bandwidth or computer capabilities to utilize an E-learning solution yet. Take care in ensuring that the infrastructure is in place before investing in E-learning training.

- **Determine the benefits of E-learning for your company**—Often people move to a new technology because it's the "latest and greatest." Investigate the benefits of E-learning for the company. If the benefits are minimal, you may want to opt out of E-learning. If the benefits aren't there, the ROI won't be there either.

- **Do a culture check**—If your company is not ready for E-learning, or the leaders of the organization are adamantly opposed to E-learning, successful implementation will be difficult.

Is E-training the Solution for You?

Look at the following considerations and questions. The answers may help to direct your E-learning decision.

Physical Location

- Where will training take place?
- Physical space
- Table space
- Desks.

What technology is available for learning?

- Internet access
- Phone lines
- Computers
- Computer capability
- Networking capabilities.

During training . . .

- What interruptions will trainees be dealing with?
- What chunks of time will they be able to afford?
- Will they have privacy?
- What is the technology comfort level of the trainees?
- How much experience do they have?
- What training have they had on using the technology?
- What is the length of training?
- What will the entire course involve?
- How many modules are there and how long are they?

Supplemental Materials and Resources

- What additional resources will you need to supply?
- What booklets, workbooks, tools, etc., will you need to provide?[3]

An Example...

A large national restaurant chain wants to improve customer service and the skills of its wait staff to increase customer satisfaction and profits.

Benefits to using E-learning:

- Consistent material is available to wait staff throughout the country.
- Materials can reflect procedures and processes specific to the restaurant chain.
- Training can happen in short, easy to remember installments.
- Managers can customize the training to individual wait staff. More experienced members may be assigned different modules than a newer person.
- You can determine the order of materials to be viewed.
- You can test wait staff on the modules, and, based on the results, direct them to more information and practice, or you can flag a manager to go over the materials with them.
- Training could happen off-site on the staff member's time if he or she has Internet access from home.
- E-learning is a low-cost investment in training for a group with high turnover.
- Many vendors provide E-learning development and maintenance services. Existing software can be easily adapted to run this program.

Drawbacks to using E-learning:

- Each restaurant would need a computer available for training that can run the program and/or access it via the Internet or a company intranet.
- Higher initial cost of training development.
- Higher cost of updating training materials.
- Maintenance of the computer system.
- Some wait staff may be intimidated by the computer and may need more instruction on how to use it.

DESIGNING E-LEARNING

Once you decide to implement E-learning in your organization, there are several factors to review, including internal or external development, the impact on your audience, and special design issues in curriculum development. E-learning is an interactive training method. To be effective, learners must be able to easily use the program with very little frustration. Learning should be designed to work with the equipment available to the user. Materials should be divided into small lessons and should have several graphic elements to engage the user. As with regular instruction, you still need to plan your goals and objectives for the training and decide how you will measure performance.

Internal or External Development

There are many companies who focus on the design and development of E-learning programs. One of the first decisions you must make is whether to use existing training or develop the training. Should you choose to develop the training, you then need to decide if you should hire a vendor to design, design it in-house, or use a combination of both.

Calculate the ROI of internal vs. external development. Look at the cost, the time commitment, quality issues, labor, and technology costs when determining the best choice of development. Refer to Appendix E for more details on calculating ROI.

Designing Instruction

Whether you decide to develop E-learning within your company or to outsource it, you need to understand the elements of E-learning.

Equipment Speed

Effective E-learning programs can turn disastrous if you have slow equipment. If you have a slow connection to the Internet, the graphic animations, video clips, and audio sounds will take longer to access and may not work properly. **Bandwidth** is the term used to measure the ability of data bits and bytes to be transmitted from place to place within a certain amount of time (usually measured in seconds). **Cable modems**, **T-1**, and **T-3 lines** provide more bandwidth and can transmit information faster. If all your computers are connected to the Internet with a 56K modem, your delivery will be slower. E-learning materials must be designed to accommodate this.

Audience Needs

The needs of your audience will drive your decisions on E-learning. Some things to consider are:

Users of E-learning will need to:

- Learn how to use self-paced training
- Become more self-disciplined
- Hold themselves accountable for their own learning.

Users of E-learning want:

- Interaction
- Relevance
- Ease of use.

Understand the key factors of E-learning, which include:

- Making it effective and appropriate to the user
- Designing it to be error free and able to run off available technology
- Using variety and creativity to design manageable modules of learning
- Incorporating a way of testing the knowledge of the learner before allowing him or her to advance to the next module
- Considering E-learning as a supplement to the total training.

TRAINER TERMS

Bandwidth -
the ability of data bits and bytes to be transmitted place to place within a certain amount of time (usually measured in seconds)

Cable Modem -
a type of modem that allows people to access the Internet via their cable television service

T-1 Line -
is a leased line (like a phone line) that is capable of carrying 1,544,000 bits per second

T-3 Line -
is a leased line (like a phone line) that is capable of carrying 44,736,000 bits per second

Structuring E-learning

Just as when we write a script for a training performance, there are some basics when developing a script for E-learning. When developing E-learning modules:

Plan Ahead

- **Examine expected outcomes or results**—What knowledge or skill do you want the audience to gain as a result of the training?

- **Don't pretend reading is training**—Don't take text from a traditional training script and drop it into an E-learning environment and believe it will be effective.

Create Modules

- **Chunk the content into 10-15 minute bites**—Break large training topics into several modules. Don't overload the audience with too much information at once.

- **Each module or chunk should be independent**—Just as in traditional training, each learning module should include a learning objective, content, and a way to measure whether the audience understood and learned the concept or skill.

- **Design the module so it is appropriate for your audience**—Consider the generation or age of the end user and design screens that are most effective for that specific audience.

- **Create modules that are interesting to view**—Use graphics, color, fonts, photos, video clips, etc., to capture and retain the interest of the learner.

- **Don't be afraid to incorporate video, animation, and audio elements**—Video, animation and audio help engage the learner and can often be the best way to measure performance or demonstrate a learned skill.

- **Ask questions frequently**—Make the module as interactive as possible by asking questions that make the learner think about the topic.

- **Build connections to other modules**—Otherwise, the learner may not see the relationship of the content in one module to that in another module.

- **Track user progress**—Build a way of tracking progress into the design of the session for both you and the learner.

Make it Easy to Use

- **Keep it simple**—Don't make the screens so complicated it takes the learner a long time to complete the module.
- **Provide very clear navigation**—If you want the audience member to go somewhere else within the system for information, make it easy to get there.

Design to Technology

- **Plan for the technology available**—If connection speeds are a concern, consider downloading data to the local computer or use CD-ROMs to hold training lessons.
- **Plan for maintenance**—Create E-learning designs that can be easily updated and changed as needed.

THE FUTURE OF E-LEARNING

As technology becomes faster and easier to use, E-learning will become a more common training method. By designing interactive, engaging materials, you can keep the attention of your audience and help them retain the information they view. New trends in technology will ensure the continued expansion of E-learning.

New Technology Trends

Several new technologies are currently being considered as delivery methods for E-learning, including:

Streaming Media via Internet

Streaming media is a live web cast that uses both audio and video. A **web cast** is a broadcast or a recording of an event over the World Wide Web using both audio and video. This allows many people to view the same information at the same time. The greatest benefit of this is the real-time dispersal of information. Think of it as a nationwide company meeting that's being held over the Internet, where everyone can attend at the same time. It is generally used for one-way communication.

TRAINER TERMS

Web cast -
a broadcast of an event, or a recording of an event, over the World Wide Web that uses both audio and video components

3-D Virtual Classroom

In an effort to engage the end user and make learning fun, a 3-D virtual classroom looks like a computer game. Each user has his or her character that navigates through a campus or a building. You can take an elevator to different classes or modules, and interact with other people who are also connected on-line. The virtual classroom is currently expensive to design, implement, and manage, but it can make learning fun and effective.

PDAs

A **PDA (Personal Digital Assistant**) is a small, hand-held device with a screen designed to track schedules, addresses, and personal information. With additional attachments, PDAs can be used to access the Internet and download information. There are several sites on the Internet that allow you to download information into your PDA. If the bandwidth of these devices can be increased, the potential for instant referencing and instant training may become a reality.

Learning Portals

A **learning portal** is a Web site where you can go to find, buy, or take E-learning courses. It provides a centralized location for finding information and training on a particular topic. Portals can deliver training to large numbers of people all over the world. While portals may offer many pre-developed E-learning courses, they may not meet your needs or address your company's business strategy. Many portal sites have hundreds of courses available, but do not have the resources to review the quality of them all. You will need high-speed Internet access to make the most of these courses.

Because of lack of time or skill, course developers and trainers often take existing text, put it into tech environment, and call it E-learning. The key is to develop the content for on-line training, using the techniques and technology available.

TECH TERMS

Asynchronous – in on-line learning, people not logged on at same time

Authoring Systems – software designed to let people create on-line learning modules that bring together text, graphics, questions, tracking, etc. They also allow you to create simulation tasks and add video, audio, and animation created by other software programs.

Bandwidth – refers to the amount of information transmitted at one time (bits and bytes per second)

Blended Learning Solutions – combines technology delivery elements with traditional training elements

Chat – discussion that occurs when two or more participants are on-line at the same time

CD-ROM – disk used to store text, audio, video, graphics, etc.

Computer-Based Training (CBT) – courses presented through technology. Courses presented on computer. Does not usually provide links to learning resources outside the course.

Cookies – files sent to a Web browser that records a user's activity on a Web site

DVD (Digital Video Disk) – disk that uses digital technology to store audio, video, etc.

Distance-learning – on-line is one form of distance-learning. Others include correspondence classes and courses by TV.

E-learning (Electronic Learning) – material presented electronically to the learner on a computer via the Internet, corporate intranet, or CD-ROM

EPSS – Electronic Performance Support Systems – software that provides performance support

Extranet – a network that is created for an organization or company but is available to people chosen by the company who may not be a part of the organization

Groupware – software that lets users send e-mail, share files, conduct on-line chats, etc. (can be synchronous or asynchronous)

Instructional Designer – person most responsible for an on-line learning project

Internet Broadcast Tools – software that lets you transmit a live presentation over the Internet

Intranet – a network only available to people who work within the company

Learning Management Systems – track student progress in a course and provides trainer with information on completion

Network – the connection of company computers located in several locations using wires and telephone or cable connections

On-Line Learning – educational materials presented on a computer

PDA (Personal Digital Assistant) – a hand-held wireless device used for a variety of functions from an electronic calendar to contact database to a way of reading e-books

Plug-in – a small piece of software that adds features to a larger piece of software

Portals – provide access to learning from multiple sources by aggregating, hosting, and distributing content

Productivity Tools – software you use in everyday work including word processing, presentation programs, database programs, and personal organizers

Software Simulation Tools – allow the end user to learn how to navigate the on-line course without an instructor

Streaming Media – the term used for continuous display of media without interruption (like a video)

Synchronous – instructor and learner are on-line at the same time

T-1 Line – is a leased line (like a phone line) that is capable of carrying 1,544,000 bits per second

T-3 Line – is a leased line (like a phone line) that is capable of carrying 44,736,000 bits per second

Technology-Based Training – refers to training through media other than the classroom, including television, computers, audiotape, videotape, and print

User Interface – used to describe the parts of a screen that a user interacts with

Web-Based Training – courses available on Internet, extranet and intranet

REFERENCES

1. Koolen, Robert. "Learning Content Management Systems - The second Wave of E-Learning." Knowledge Mechanics, Internet Article. August 2001.

2. Moran, John. "Top 10 E-learning Myths." T&D. September 2000. p. 33.

3. Kaeter, Margaret. "Virtual Cap & Gown." Training. September 2000. pp. 115 - 122.

SKILL BUILDERS

1. Develop a memo to an organization explaining E-learning and how it can assist in improving training within the organization.

2. Create an organization audit form for reviewing the hardware, software and technical support available for an E-learning program. Be sure to include the Internet access, power of the network or individual machines, and the capacity for more than one person at a time to participate.

3. Take an existing mini-lecture and outline the modification and media needs for turning it into an E-learning module.

APPENDIX A

RESOURCES - BOOKS, PERIODICALS, AND OTHERS

Research is changing everyday. How do you keep up? Where do you go to keep up on the changes? In the words of the great Dr. Suess:

"The places I hiked to!

The roads that I rambled

To find the best eggs that

have ever been scrambled!

If you want to get eggs you

can't buy at a store,

You have to do things

never thought of before."

In an effort to help you in your quest for continuous improvement, the following pages are filled with resources to investigate.

BOOKS

301 Ways to Have Fun at Work. Dave Hemsath & Leslie Yerkes. Berrett-Koehler Publishers, Inc. San Francisco. 1997.

Active Training: A Handbook of Techniques, Designs, Case Examples and Tips. By Mell Silberman and Carol Averback. Pfeiffer & Co. 1998.

The Art of Possibility: Transforming Professional and Personal Life. Rosamund Stone Zander and Benjamin Zander. Harvard Business School Press. Boston. 2000

The ASTD Handbook of Training Design and Delivery. George M. Piskurich. McGraw-Hill. 1999.

Beep! Beep! Competing in the Age of the Road Runner. Chip R. Bell and Oren Harari. Warner Books. 2000.

The Complete Idiot's Guide to Business Etiquette. Mary Mitchell with John Corr. Macmillan USA, Inc. Indianapolis. 2000.

The Complete Games Trainers Play. Edward E. Scannell and John W. Newstrom. McGraw-Hill, Inc. New York. 1994.

The Complete Games Trainers Play, Volume II. Edward E. Scannell and John W. Newstrom. McGraw-Hill, Inc. New York. 1998.

The Complete Games Trainers Play: Experiential Learning Exercises. Edward E. Scannell and John W. Newstrom with Carolyn D Nilson. McGraw-Hill, Inc. New York. 1998.

Creating Your Career Portfolio:At a Glance Guide. Anna Graf Williams and Karen Hall. Prentice Hall. 2001.

Designing Web-based Training. William R. Horton. John Wiley & Sons. 2000.

Multimedia-Based Instructional Design. William W. Lee and Diana L. Owens. Jossey-Bass. 2000.

The Disney Way. Bill Capadagli and Lynn Jackson. McGraw Hill. 1998.

E-Learning: Strategies for Delivering Knowledge in the Digital Age. Marc J. Rosenberg. New York. McGraw–Hill. 2001.

Evaluating Training Programs: The Four Levels. Berrett-Koehler Publishers. San Francisco. 1996.

The Experience Economy. Joseph Pine, James H. Gilmore, and B. Joseph Pine II. Harvard Business School Press. 1999.

Generations at Work: Managing the Clash of Veterans, Boomers, Xers, and Nexters in Your Workplace. Ron Zemke, Claire Raines, Bob Filipczak. AMACON. 2000.

Human Possibilities: Human Capital in the 21st Century. Robert R. Carkhiff. Human Resource Development Press. 2000.

Making Training Stick. Dora Johnson, Ed.D, and Barbara Carnes, Ph.D. 1988.

Making Training Stick: A Training Transfer Field Guide. Dora Johnson, Ed.D, and Barbara Carnes, Ph.D. 1994.

An Overview of On-line Learning. Saul Carliner. Human Resources Development Press. 1999.

Return On Investment: In training and performance improvement programs. Jack J. Phillips. Gulf Publishing Company. Houston. 1997.

Running Training Like A Business. David Van Adelsberg and Edward A. Trolly. Berrett-Koehler Publishing. 1999.

Simplicity: In a World of Better, Quicker, Faster. Bill Jensen. Perseus. 2000.

The Soul at Work: Listen…Respond…Let go. Roger Lewin and Birute Regine. Simon & Schuster. 2000.

The Story Factor: Inspiration Influence and Persuasion Through the Art of Storytelling. Annett Simmons. Perseus Books. Cambridge .2001.

ThinkerToys. Michael Michalko. Ten Speed Press. 1991.

Tools & Activities for a Diverse Workforce. Anthony Patrick Carnevale & S. Kanu Kogod Editors. McGraw-Hill, Inc. New York. 1996.

Training From the Heart. Barry Lyerly and Cyndi Maxey. ASTD. 2001.

The Training Needs Analysis Toolkit. Sharon Bartram and Brenda Gilson. Human Resource Development Press. 2000.

Trainers in Motion: Creating a Participant-Centered Learning Experience. Jim Vidakovich. AMACOM. 2000.

Turning Training Into Learning: How to Design and Deliver Programs that Get Results. Sheila W. Furjanic and Laurie A. Trotman. AMACOM. 2000.

The Ultimate Training Workshop. McGraw-Hill. 1999.

Wow! How Did They Think of That? Ted Coulson and Alison Strickland. Applied Creativity Inc., 2000.

PERIODICALS TO CHECK OUT

"Managing Training & Development"

Published by the Institute of Management and Administration, Inc.

212-244-0360

"Creative Training Techniques"

Published by Bill Communications.

800-328-4329 Ext. 4805

"Training Directors' Forum Newsletter"

800-328-4329

"First Draft"

800-878-5331

"Soundview Executive Book Summaries"

800-521-1227

DIGITAL STOCK PHOTOGRAPHY

- Media Image Resource Alliance – 978-739-9022

MUSIC

- Broadcast Music Inc. – 212-586-2000
- Harry Fox Agency – 212-586-5330

VIDEO

■ Motion Picture Licensing Corp. – 800-462-8855

CARTOONS

■ United Media – 212-293-8500
■ Universal Press Syndication – 816-932-6600

This list is not meant to be all inclusive, nor is it meant to represent this author's opinion of what is the best out there. The author has neither business relationships nor any affiliation with any of the products, companies, etc., listed. They are presented for the purpose of providing you with potential resources.

APPENDIX B

ON-LINE RESOURCES

BOOK AND BINDER VENDORS

- www.barnesandnoble.com
- www.amazon.com
- HRDQ—800-633-4533—www.HRDQ.com
- AMACOM—800-262-9699—www.amacombooks.org
- www.amanet.org/books
- ASTD Press—800-628-2783—www.astd.org
- Harvard Business School Press—800-988-0886
- Jossey-Bass Publishers—800-956-7739—www.jbp.com
- Prentice-Hall—800-922-0579—www.pearsonptr.com

ON-LINE LEARNING COMPANIES

- www.Click2learn.com
- www.Smartplanet.com
- www.Edupoint.com
- www.Geolearning.com
- www.Emind.com
- www.Hungryminds.com
- www.Headlight.com
- www.Elearners.com
- www.Trainingnet.com

- www.Knowledgeplanet.com
- www.Brandon-hall.com
- www.techsmith.com

Cool Web Sites

- www.trainingsupersite.com
- www.humorproject.com
- www.simplerwork.com/library
- www.franklincovey.com
- www.learnativity.com
- www.fastcompany.com
- www.fool.com
- www.presentations.com
- www.workforceonline.com
- www.lookatmorestuff.com
- www.trainingmag.com
- www.learningcircuits.org
- www.trainingsite.com
- www.sstcommuniications.com—Theater-based training
- www.Rfp.thinq.com—RFP Exchange

Resources for On-Line Info on On-Line Learning Design

- www.hotwired.com
- www.info.med.yale.-edu/caim/manual
- www.webreview.com
- www.i5ive.com

- www.learnativity.com
- www.ebrainware-tm.com/catalog.htm
- On Animation—www.3dchor.com

SOFTWARE COMPANIES

- Macromedia Dreamweaver
- Macromedia Director
- Macromedia Shockwave
- Macromedia Flash
- Adobe Go Live
- Microsoft Frontpage
- Quicktime

COMPANIES FOR PROMOTIONAL ITEMS/ TRAINING AIDS

- Best impression—www.bestimpression.com
- Goldleaf Promotional Products—www.goldleaf.com
- Idea Art—www.ideaart.com

VIDEO VENDORS

- Charthouse Learning – 800-328-3789

ORGANIZATIONS TO CHECK OUT

- American Society of Training and Development (ASTD)—www.astd.org
- Council of Hotel and Restaurant Trainers (CHART)—www.chart.org
- International Council on Hospitality and Tourism Education (CHRIE)—www.chrie.org
- Society of Human Resource Professionals (SHRM)—www.shrm.org

FOR INFORMATION ON GAMES, CHECK OUT THESE WEB SITES

- Workshops by Thiagi: Free on-line puzzles, games, tips, etc.
    www.Thiagi.com
- Society for Advancement of Games & Simulations
    www.ms.ic.ac.uk/sagset
- North American Simulation & Gaming Association
    www.nasaga.org
- The Trainer's Warehouse – 800-299-3770
    www.trainerswarehouse.com
- Tool Thyme for Trainers – For catalogue, call: 504-887-5558
    www.tool-trainers.com
- Bob Pike Group – 800-383-9210
    www.bobpikegroup.com

This list is not meant to be all-inclusive, nor is it meant to represent this author's opinion of what is the best out there. The author has neither business relationships nor any affiliation with any of the products, companies, etc., listed. They are presented for the purposes of providing you with potential resources.

APPENDIX C

TRAINING TIP ON COPYRIGHTS

If you find the perfect quote, video, or cartoon, be sure to obtain permission from the powers that be:

- Library of Congress, U.S. Copyright Office:
    - www.lcweb.loc.gov/copyright

For print materials:

- Copyright Clearance Center, Danvers, MA – 978-750-8400
    - www.copyright.com

APPENDIX D

THE NEW TRAINING ROOM

HOW WE LEARN

One very exciting area of research in training is the examination of the link between mind and body in an effort to gain insight into how humans learn. In her article "The Mind-Body Connection in Learning" (TD, September, 2001, pp. 61-70), Ruth Palombo Weiss offers some interesting insight. She quotes Dr. John Ratey that "many of the fundamental tools for nurturing the brain are everyday matters. We all know that proper nutrition, exercise – physical and mental – and sufficient sleep help us remain sharp cognitively and steady emotionally." There are also many studies linking the brain to the body. Brain research indicates "physical movement affects thought."

Jeff Barbian, in his article "RE: Training Room" (Training, September, 2001 pp. 41-45), explores various new technologies that could change how training is delivered and how people learn.

Lucid Dreaming

Lucid dreaming occurs when you are dreaming intensely and vividly. Research from both the Lucidity Institute and Stanford University has focused on the possibilities surrounding lucid dreaming. Stephen LaBerge of Lucidity Institute is quoted saying "Research on how to cultivate peak performance suggests that lucid dreaming may prove to be an ideal training ground, not only for athletics, but also for any area in which skill can be developed."

Tele-immersion

Tele-immersion is "a technology that would provide high-fidelity, life-sized, holographic projections in which you'd see and hear remote collaborators as plainly as if they were there in the office." This could have tremendous applications in training rooms and offices around the world.

Virtual Retinal Display

Virtual Retinal Display or VRD technology developed at the University of Washington "takes what you see on a monitor and compacts it through special glasses directly on the retina in a full-color, high-resolution, wide field-of-view screen. The image looks like it's floating directly in front of you at about arm's length and can be used in any or even no light source." Matt Nichols, director of communications for Microvision, the commercial developer of VRD, says "It redefines on-the-job training, and unlike virtual reality, the devices don't shut out the real world."

Digital Pedagogy

Barbian's article goes on to focus on how software and digital technology will change how an individual learns. He quotes futurist Barry Minkin, suggesting, "Human/computer interfaces will create ultra-accessible intelligent tutoring systems that understand your learning patterns and offer up content designed and delivered according." It goes on to discuss Macromedia's Flash as a development tool that "Nunica, Mass.-based Media 1 has used to develop virtual teachers for on-line instruction." Using its "Flash Avatar" application, corporate trainers can fashion detailed, animated versions of themselves to facilitate sessions over low-bandwidth connections. The animated avatars are graced with an instructor's actual voice and mannerisms; unlike the human version, avatar-led classes and help sessions would be available around the clock.

Extras

In addition to those above, there is a great deal of interest and research being done in areas of:

- Knowledge management which deals with information sharing
- Corporate-college partnerships, focusing on the evolving relationship of the academy and business, which is becoming more of a partnership than ever before

- Accelerated learning which investigates techniques that allow the learner to learn more quickly

- NLP or neuro linguistics programming, which deals with psychological skills and memory.

Whether it's technology or learning technique, one thing is certain; changes are inevitable and the face of training will need to change with it.

APPENDIX E

WRITING A PROPOSAL

WRITING A PROPOSAL

An integral part of the training process is writing a training proposal. A proposal includes an outline of the training to be conducted, justification as to why, targeted audience, estimated length of training, how it will be conducted, how much the initiative will cost, and how long it will take. For most organizations, training proposals are required when:

- The expense exceeds set limits
- The training involves many people
- The training involves a company-wide initiative
- The training introduces a new business practice

There are some organizations, however, that expect a proposal for every training program developed. When a training proposal is expected, it needs to be submitted and approved before you begin any design.

PART ONE: THE DESCRIPTION

The key components of a proposal are:

- Purpose of the proposal
  This is a one- to three-paragraph summary, describing the training you are proposing. Be as concise and clear as possible in defining both what training you are proposing and why you are proposing it.

- Who will benefit from the training or who will be trained
  The next part of the proposal should explain or identify the benefits of the training: who it will benefit and how it will benefit them. This can be one sentence to one page depending on what you are trying to communicate.

- The measurable goals and objectives of the training
  Identify the goals and objectives developed for the training. Include the measurement tools that will be used to measure effectiveness of the training. Be specific.

- How much the training will cost and what the Return on the Investment is projected to be.

- How long it will take or what the timeline is for the Return on Investment. This is a one paragraph summary. The details of how the amounts were derived will be described in Part Two of the proposal.

- A timeline from planning through execution
  This timeline needs to include development time, planning time, delivery of the training, and any followup measurements or post-work.

- How the proposed activity will be introduced to the company
  This includes the process for rolling out the training, a list of individuals who will be needed to help support the process, and any other resources that will be needed.

- Any benchmarking you have done to support the training
  Finally, any information, competitive comparisons, etc., that you have done as part of the Needs Analysis should be included here.

PART TWO: THE FINANCIAL IMPACT

This section of the proposal deals with the costs associated with training, the benefits/savings as a direct result of the training, and Cost/Benefit Ratio or Return on Investment calculations. The more detailed the financial information, the stronger the case for doing the training. It's important to be as accurate as possible. Remember omission of details or manipulation of the data is equal to stealing or, at the very least, is unethical.

First identify all the costs of the project you are proposing. Specific examples of the breakdown of costs include:

- Cost of development time
- Cost of reference materials, licenses, etc.
- Cost of participant guides/handouts, facilitator guide
- Cost of any audio visual materials like videotapes

- Cost of room, meals, equipment rentals, or purchases, etc.
- Cost of trainer's salary, lodging, food, travel, etc.
- Cost of any shipping of materials, etc.
- Cost of new technology required, etc.

Once you have identified the costs, the next step is to look at the savings or benefits that will be experienced as a direct result of the project you are proposing.   Keep in mind that while most benefits need to be shown in financial terms, there are times when the benefits are "soft" or less quantifiable. They are, however, just as important to list. Specific examples of savings or benefits the company will realize include:

- Savings on salaries
- Increased customer satisfaction
- More efficient operations
- Lower turnover
- Higher profitability
- Increased goodwill.

PART THREE: THE ROI

Using the formula discussed in detail in Chapter Ten, calculate the proposed Return on Investment for the proposal. In your final analysis also include length of time for the ROI to be realized (i.e., six months, one year, two years, etc.). In this section, very clearly display:

- Total cost of the proposed training project
- Total savings as a result of doing the training
- Total Return on Investment of doing the training project of the proposal.

If the proposal involves many expenses and details over a long period of time, you may want to consider doing a budget for the project or proposal. If you choose to do this, submit the budget with your proposal. Chapter Ten also provides details on the budgeting process.

There is no specific format for a proposal. However, the more detailed your information, the better your chance of getting it approved. Make sure you have all the facts. Prepare yourself so you can answer any questions anyone might have. Don't assume that just because you believe in the proposal everyone will. It's your job to sell them on the benefits!

When writing out the proposal, use headings throughout the document. Also, if it is over five pages in length, provide a Table of Contents for ease of reading.

GLOSSARY

Actor - the trainer on the stage of the training performance

Asynchronous - in on-line learning, people not logged on at same time

Audience - the participants (employees, managers, etc.) who come to the training performance

Audio/Visual (A/V) - an aid, other than printed matter, that uses sight or sound to present information

Authoring systems - software designed to let people create on-line learning modules and simulation tasks

Bandwidth - a data transmission rate; the maximum amount of information (bits/second) that can be transmitted along a channel

Banquet tables - tables that are 6 feet long by 30 inches wide used primarily for U- or square-shaped setups

Bells & Whistles - anything added to enhance presentation (graphics, pictures, sound, color, backgrounds, etc.)

Benchmark - a standard by which something can be measured or judged

Best practice - organization's procedures or practices that outline the "best" way to perform a task

Blended learning solutions - combine technology delivery elements with traditional training elements

Brainstorming - a method of shared problem solving in which all members of a group spontaneously contribute ideas, all are recorded, none are rejected, and ideas build upon each other

Business need - A condition or situation in which something is required or wanted by an organization

Cable modem - A type of modem that allows people to access the Internet via their cable television service

CD-ROM - a compact disk that is used with a computer (rather than with an audio system); a large amount of digital information can be stored and accessed but it cannot be altered by the user

Chat - an on-line discussion that occurs between two or more participants

Classroom-style tables - tables that are typically 4 feet long by 18 inches wide used primarily for classroom style setup

Co-facilitating - when both performers work together to make the training process easier by interacting simultaneously within the training experience

Computer-Based Training (CBT) - courses presented on a computer that are usually not linked to learning resources outside the course

Cookies - a collection of information, usually including a user name and the current date and time, stored on the local computer of a person using the World Wide Web, used chiefly by Web sites to identify users who have previously registered or visited the site

Co-presenting - where each trainer introduces, offers expertise and/or consideration on the training content jointly

Copyright - the legal right granted to an author, composer, playwright, publisher, or distributor to exclusive publication, production, sale, or distribution of a literary, musical, dramatic, or artistic work

Cue videotapes - to position (an audio or video recording) in readiness for playing

Defining moments - the moments throughout a person's life that have made a significant impact on who that person is and how they think (Zemke's "Generations at Work")

Demographics - the characteristics of human populations and population segments. It includes facts such as geographic origin, cultural background, age, gender, etc

Demonstrable assessments - a skill test in which the trainer watches the audience member demonstrate the new skill; typically uses some type of checklist or set of criteria as a measurement tool

Developer - the person that designs the content of a training performance

Discovery learning - type of learning in which the learner, through a series of questions or activities, seeks out answers and information from books, observations, or other methods

Distance learning - education in which students take academic courses by accessing information and communicating with the instructor asynchronously over a computer network. Also called distance education.

Dress rehearsal - a full rehearsal shortly before the first performance

DVD (Digital Video Disk) - a high-density compact disk for storing large amounts of data, especially high-resolution audio-visual material

Edutainment/Trainertainment - education and training that has been combined with a type of entertainment element

E-learning (Electronic Learning) - learning where the material is presented electronically on a computer via the Internet, corporate intranet, or CD-ROM

Energizer - a short activity designed to increase the energy level of the audience

EPSS (Electronic Performance Support Systems) - software that provides performance support

Etiquette - rules governing socially acceptable behavior that can make a significant impact on the effectiveness of a training performance

Evaluation (student) - student's appraisal of the training performance

Extranet - an extension of an institution's intranet, especially over the World Wide Web, enabling communication between the institution and people it deals with, often by providing limited access to its intranet

F&B (food and beverage) - food and beverages, which may be contracted for, during breaks and meals

Facilitator guides - guide that contains the content that needs to be covered by the trainer during the class

Facilitator or trainer - one who trains; an instructor who makes learning easier

Fast track learners - a person or persons who learn rapidly

Formative evaluation - the evaluation you do during a session can help you revise your training while in process

Game - a structured activity with a specific learning objective at the end

Gap - the difference between current performance level of an employee and the level that is required to be successful

Gestures - a motion of the limbs or body made to express or help express thought or to emphasize speech

Goal - the purpose toward which an endeavor is directed; an objective; goals are used to set direction and frame your activities

Group training - a method of training involving three or more people being trained simultaneously

Groupware - software that integrates work on a single project by several concurrent users at separated workstations

Hard skills - specific skills that involve completing tasks or something you physically do

Icebreakers - activities done to relax a formal atmosphere or situation usually involving the entire group

In and Out thinking - the concept that the conscious mind will wander on and off the topic being discussed

In-house - training conducted in a training room or classroom located within the company's building or site

Instructional designer - person most responsible for an on-line learning project

Internet - an interconnected system of networks that connects computers around the world

Internet broadcast tools - software that lets you transmit a live presentation over the Internet

Intranet - a privately maintained computer network that can be accessed only by authorized persons, especially members or employees of the organization that owns it

Just-in-time learning - allows learners to learn at their own pace, when it is convenient for them

Just-in-time training - quick response training delivered at the moment it is needed

Key stakeholders - a person or persons that directly impact the organization and its success

Kinesics - the study of bodily movement; a large part of nonverbal communication

Learning management systems - track student progress and provide information on completion

Learning objectives - specific, clear, and measurable descriptors that indicate how to reach your goals

Learning portal - a Web site where you can find, buy, or take E-learning courses

Logistics coordinator - traditionally focuses on the mechanics of tuition, training costs, materials, salary and wages, room rental, audio/visual, shipping, licensing fees, travel, and charge-backs, which surround training

Logistics of training - the details including. time, place, registration, room setup, audio/visual, and food and beverage

Needs analysis - a process used to identify gaps or needs between the current state and desired state in the organization so appropriate training can be developed to improve organizational performance

Network - interconnected or intersecting configuration or system of components

Nonverbal communication - communication without the use of words

Norms - behaviors or accepted practices agreed upon by the group prior to a training performance

Number guaranteed - a final count or final number of people that will be attending an event

Off-the-shelf - training modules or training programs which someone else has developed that many different companies can purchase

On-line learning - education materials presented on a computer that links to learning resources outside the course

Participant - a student or employee who will be attending a traditional training class

Participant manuals - manuals and guides used to help the student throughout the class: they serve as a workbook during training and as a reference back in the workplace

PDA (Personal Digital Assistant) - a lightweight, hand-held, usually pen-based computer used as a personal organizer

Performance - the act or style of performing a work or role before an audience

Performance checks - checks used to determine if the audience members are learning the content

Playwright - the person who develops a storyline into a script. In training, the playwright is the person developing the training topic or the storyline into the training script.

Plug-in - a small piece of software that adds features to a larger piece of software

Portals - provide access to learning from multiple sources by aggregating, hosting, and distributing content

Post-work - allows the trainee to reinforce what was learned and utilize it when he or she is back on the job

Preparation - the state of having been made ready beforehand; readiness. Preparing for training includes getting materials ready, checking logistics, and preparing to present.

Pre-work - allows the trainee to "ramp-up" for training by gaining information on the subject before coming to class

Producer - one who supervises and controls the finances, creation, and public presentation of a play, film, program, or similar work

Productivity tools - software used in everyday work, including word processing, presentation programs, and database programs and personal organizers

Proposal - request for a training performance which includes an outline of the training to be conducted, justification as to why the training is needed, the targeted audience, the estimated length of training, how it will be conducted, and how much the initiative will cost

Registered trademark - a name, symbol, or other device identifying a product, officially registered and legally restricted to the use of the owner or manufacturer

Return on Investment (ROI) - the measurement or an actual value developed by comparing program costs to benefits

Reviews - in training, the evaluations that help the actor improve

Room capacity - the maximum number of people a room can hold

Root cause - the main reason a problem exists

Round tables - tables that are typically 60 inches, 72 inches, or 90 inches

Script - the story the actors bring to life for the audience

Simulation exercises - a game that attempts to accurately recreate a situation, on a large or small scale

Smile sheets - a reaction sheet or a "mini-survey" designed to survey the audience

Soft skills - skills that are less tangible or concrete

Software simulation tools - allow the end user to learn how to navigate the on-line course without an instructor

Stage - the environment in which the trainer performs

Sticky training - training that can be recalled and utilized by the learner

Storyline - the idea or topic that will be woven into a training performance

Streaming media - continuous display of media without interruption

Subject Matter Expert (SME) - someone who has expert knowledge about a given topic or skill

Summative evaluation - evaluation completed at the end of a training performance that demonstrates skills or knowledge

Symptom - a sign or an indication of disorder

Synchronous - when the instructor and learner are on-line at the same time

T-1 Line - is a leased line (like a phone line) that is capable of carrying 1,544,000 bits per second

T-3 Line - is a leased line (like a phone line) that is capable of carrying 44,736,000 bits per second

Technology-based training - training through media, other than the classroom, including television, computers, audiotape, videotape, and print

Traditional instructional design (TID) - a detailed process for identifying and developing training

Training - a dynamic process among people that focuses on the exchange of ideas, with a spirit toward learning and continuous improvement

Training class - a method of delivering information to learners

Training moment - an interaction between the trainer and the trainee where the trainer has observed a behavior and is communicating how the trainee can improve upon it

Training room - the place where a facilitator or trainer delivers training to learners

Training topic - the subject identified as a need for training or personal development

Transfer of learning - skills or knowledge the trainee has learned and can perform or use in the workplace

User-friendly - easy for the user to access, read, and understand; they are well organized and appropriate for the level of the audience

User interface - used to describe the parts of a screen that a user interacts with

Web-based training - courses available on Internet, extranet, and intranet

Web cast - a broadcast of an event, or a recording of an event, over the World Wide Web that uses both audio and video components

What's In It For Me? (WIIFM) - describes the benefit of the activity or action being discussed

Windowpane - a summary sheet for training, often including topics, key points, length of time, goals, and content

Written tests - tests that can include true/false statements, multiple-choice questions, fill-in-the-blank questions, or essay questions; used for testing technical information that needs to be memorized

INDEX

A

acronyms 40
activities 112
actor 6, 37–50
   - See also trainer
   energy level 45
   listening skills 45
   role of 38
   script 125
adult learning principles xvi, 54, 93, 107
age diversity 3
agenda 175
announcements 149
appearance 44
audience
   capturing attention 5
   communicating with 38
   diversity 3
   engaging the 93
   greeting the 170
   identifying 54, 146
   needs 208
   notifying about training 148–150
   participants 7
   size 113
audience attention 5
audio/visual equipment 7, 96–102, 144
   comparison chart 102
   day of performance 165
   high-tech 99
   low-tech 97
   planning for 162
   preparation 129, 175
   rehearsing with 163
   summary chart 102
   uses in room 142

B

baby boomers 59
bandwidth 207
bells & whistles 101
benchmarking 18, 131
best practice 24
Bloom Taxonomy 70
brainstorming 12, 63, 65
brainteasers 103
breaks 145
brown bag 78
business goals 189
business need 12

C

cable modems 207
candy 103
case studies 28
CD player 100, 102, 143
CD-ROM 202
certification tests 188
chalkboards 97, 102
checklist 161
closing 176
closing session 117
coaching 189
co-facilitating 167
competencies 184
computer-based training 202
conflicts 173
content outline 63, 65
contracts 150
   additional fees 151
   cancellation policy 150
   final count date 150
   room rental costs 150

contracts (cont'd.)
    room rental discounts 150
co-presenting 167
copyrights 131
cultural diversity 3

D

data collection 17
defining moments 58
demographics 56
demonstrable assessments 26
developer 6
digital cameras 143
discovery learning 81
distance-learning 202
distraction 172
dress rehearsal 8
dry erase board - See whiteboard

E

E-book 83
edutainment 4
E-learning
    structuring 209
e-mail 149
emotion and learning 93
energizers 95
enhancing the script 7
ESL (English as a second language) - See
        audience, primary language
ethics 122, 131
etiquette 48
evaluations 8
experiential levels 164
eye contact 43

F

facilitator - See actor
facilitators
    outside 128

facility
    type of 135
fast track learners 160
feedback 190
flip charts 97, 102, 129, 142
        electronic 99, 102
        preparing 162
flyers/posters 149
focus group 17
food and beverage 144, 150
        breakfast 145
        counts 150
        discounts 150
        low budget 145
        lunch 145
formative evaluation 31

G

gallery walk 98
games 110
generational differences 58
Generations at Work 58, 124
Generation X 59
gestures 43
goals 20, 62

H

hard skills 80

I

icebreakers 114, 175
in and out thinking 172
inspections 187
instructional design 32
interactive storytelling 107
Internet 202
intranet 202
invitations 148

J

jargon 123
jitters 170
job analysis 32
just-in-time learning 203
just-in-time training 83

K

key stakeholders 13, 16
kinesics 42

L

laser pointer 143
LCD projector 101, 102, 143
learner-centered approach 128
learning objectives 21, 23, 33, 62, 69, 184
learning portals 211
listening skills 45
logistics coordinator 6
logistics of training 8

M

marketing 145–148
master list 152
measurement 4, 24–31, 64, 90, 180–184
    - See also return on investment
    against standards 185
    business goals, against 189
    competencies 184
    continuous 190
    example 190–192
    goals 232
    in goals 21
    in script 64
    Kirkpatrick evaluation
        model 180–181
    objectives 21, 69, 184, 232
    performance-based 182–183
    pre and post test 31
    standards of performance 23

measurement (cont'd.)
    tests 26
    tools 30
    types of 26
memory and learning 93
memos 149
mind mapping 66
multiple-day performances 175
music, using 100

N

needs analysis 16–19, 20, 21, 22
    analyze data 18
    data collection 17
    example of 22
    goal setting 69
    set priorities 19
    steps in 17
new workplace xvi, 2, 58
    measuring success in 182
Nexter 59
nonverbal communication 42
norms 114
number guaranteed 150

O

observation checklists 186
off-the-shelf training 31, 85, 163
on-line learning 202
opening session 114
outline - See script
overhead projector 97, 102
    screen 142

P

Parking Lot 164
participant
    - See audience 7
participant handbook
    - See audience, script 122

PDA 211
peer mentoring 80
performance 8
    checklist 161
performance, contd.
    checks 26
    conflicts during 173
    data 17
    day 165
    elements of 64, 90
    flow of 95
    multiple-day 175
    scheduling 134
    standards 184
performance-based training 182
physical plant 174
pilot test 33
playwright 6
post-performance 154
PowerPoint® 98, 129
    using 101
preparation 8
pre-/post-work 78
problem solving 15
producer 6
projectors
    LCD 101
    rear screen 101, 102
proposals
    creating 13
    defined 13
    writing 231–234
props 64, 104, 122, 161

Q

qualitative 18
quality audits 187
quantitative 18
questions 171
    answering 50

    anticipating 159
    as a listening tool 46
    asking 46
    rules for asking 116

R

recognition 72
registered trademarks 131
registration 147, 152
return on investment 2, 193–??
    calculating 195
    defined 193
    e-training 207
    proposals, in 232–233
reviews 8
ROI - See return on investment
role-play exercises 27, 112
room setup 140
    classroom style 140
    rounds 141
    square 141
    theater style 140
    U-shape 141
root causes 13

S

script 7, 62
    actor's 64, 122, 125
        layout 125
    audience 64, 122
    audits 186
    outline 70
    writing 119
script writing
    at-a-glance guide 63–64
secret shoppers 187
self-confidence 50
setting the stage 8
simulation exercises 29
smile sheets 180

soft skills training 78
stage 7
    capacity 136
    color 137
    decor 138
    layout 137
    lighting 138
    selecting 134
    setup 139
standards of performance 23, 62
sticky training 4, 91
storyboarding 66
storyline 7, 12
    development process 12
subject matter expert (SME) 73
summative evaluation 31
symptom 15

T

T-1 lines 207
T-3 lines 207
technology 3, 129, 202
telephone audits 186
toys, uses in training 105
trainer
    - See also actor
    answering questions 50
    appearance 44
    guide 122
    guides 7
    preparation 49
trainertainment 4
training 6–8
    - See also performance
    activities 112
    class 8
    closing 176
    closing session 117
    creativity 108
    defined 2

group 83
humor 106
interruptions 120
making it fun 103
methods 63
moments 82
norms 114
one-on-one 79
opening 114
room 7
schedule 63, 74
self-directed 81
sticky 91
through technology 82
time for 77
topics 7
traditional 6–8
types of 79, 84
with impact 4
training as performance 6–8
transfer of learning 4
transparencies 97, 102, 129
troubleshooting 174
TV 100, 143

U

user-friendly 123

V

VCR 143
veterans 58
video 100, 102, 130
    animated 105
    cuing tapes 165
video camera 143

W

web cast 210
weekend seminars 77
What's In It For Me? (WIIFM) 55

whiteboard 97, 102
    electronic 99, 102
    interactive 99, 102
windowpane 126
written tests 26

Z

Zemke, Ron 58–59, 124, 201